Juicing

AND

Smoothies
Quick & Easy
Proven Recipes

014183210 7

Publisher's Note: Raw or semi-cooked eggs should not be consumed by babies, toddlers, pregnant or breastfeeding women, the elderly or those suffering from a recurring illness.

Publisher and Creative Director: Nick Wells
Senior Project Editor: Laura Bulbeck
Art Director: Mike Spender
Layout Design: Jane Ashley
Digital Design & Production: Chris Herbert
Special thanks to Catherine Taylor and Frances Bodiam.

FLAME TREE PUBLISHING
6 Melbray Mews
Fulham, London SW6 3NS
United Kingdom

www.flametreepublishing.com

This edition first published 2017

17 19 21 20 18
1 3 5 7 9 10 8 6 4 2

© 2017 Flame Tree Publishing Ltd

A CIP record for this book is available from the British Library upon request.

ISBN: 978-1-78664-475-6

Printed in China | Created, Developed & Produced in the United Kingdom

All images are courtesy of **Flame Tree Publishing Ltd** except the following, which are courtesy of **Shutterstock.com** and © the following: line drawings: Monash; 14 Catalin Petolea; 15 Fatseyeva; 16 Vitaly Korovin; 17t Cloud7Days; 17c R3BV; 17b JIANG HONGYAN; 18c Thalinee Prakobthong; 18b Tim UR; 19t Dionisvera; 19br Nattstudio. All illustrations are courtesy Shutterstock.com.

Juicing

AND

Smoothies
Quick & Easy
Proven Recipes

General Editor: Gina Steer

**FLAME TREE
PUBLISHING**

Contents

Introduction

❀

Orange juice

We all know that we need to improve our diets by eating more fruit and vegetables and, indeed, many people have taken this to heart and have already increased their intake. The World Health Organization recommends that we eat at least five portions of fruit and vegetables per day. However, for some, this is not as easy as it sounds, due to lifestyle, taste or even economics.

Healthy Eating

Life is hectic for many people and often involves eating on the go, grabbing a bite as we rush from place to place and seldom managing to eat healthily. There is also a question of taste. We may not like some or all vegetables or even fruit. Children in particular are often fussy and 'picky' eaters, and sometimes when they say, 'I don't like this', it is easier just to take it away and not force the issue. In addition, fresh fruits and vegetables can sometimes be expensive, pushing the family budget too high.

This is where fruit juices and smoothies are the perfect answer. You can make healthy and delicious drinks, with no added extras such as sugar, colourings or preservatives, out of one or two fruits or vegetables for next to nothing. These will still provide a delicious drink crammed full of vitamins, minerals and fibre. The fruits and vegetables used for juicing need not be uniform and perfect in size, as long as they are undamaged by bruising or are not going rotten. They will work perfectly, with an added benefit of being ready in no time at all – ideal for when the children come in tired and thirsty or you need a quick energy boost.

One of the biggest benefits of consuming fruit is the advantage it gives you in the fight against cancer and heart disease, two of the biggest killers in the twenty-first century throughout the western world. Many fruits contain antioxidants, a vital component against these problems. Fruit and vegetables can also give you extra natural energy as well as keeping your immune system alert and strong. So it really does make sense to include more of these vital ingredients into your diet and that of your family.

Getting Started

When it comes to ingredients that are suitable, there are very few limits. Most fruits are suitable providing they are ripe and juicy. With vegetables it is more of a question of personal taste than the vegetable itself, as most can be made into a delicious, if unusual, drink. Herbs and spices can also be incorporated. If using herbs, many of which have great health benefits, remember to check that they are thoroughly cleaned with no aphids or other creepy crawlies. Spices with hard outer casing will need either pounding or cracking open in a pestle and mortar to release the seeds.

Let's not forget that juices and especially smoothies do not have to be the healthy option – they can be sweet and tasty or indulgent drinks. This book contains a fabulous selection of recipes ranging from simple fruit or vegetable juices and delicious creamy smoothies, to drinks designed to lift and revitalize, others to help in healthy detoxification, and some rather more decadent concoctions. Adapt the recipes to suit your taste, substituting ingredients if necessary. After a couple of weeks, you will be happily juicing and smoothing at every opportunity.

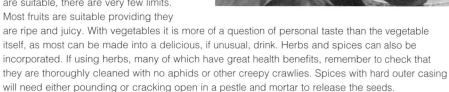

The Basics

This book is packed full of tempting recipes for all sorts of occasions – whether you want to use up some leftover fruit and veg to make a healthy drink, or are looking to create something extra special. To get you started, here is some advice on the basic equipment you'll be needing as well as which ingredients you'll commonly want and how best to prepare them.

Equipment AND Tips

Equipment and Utensils

These days, we enjoy a vast array of fruit and vegetables, ranging from home-grown varieties to tropical produce. In order to be able to prepare and make the recipes in this book, it would be useful to own certain pieces of equipment and utensils.

∽ Juicer: This is a simple machine that will extract the juice from fruit or vegetables while leaving the skin, pulp, seeds and debris behind. All fruits and vegetables can be juiced, including parsnips, carrots, cabbage, beetroots, apples, pineapples, oranges and melons. Juicers come in three types:

Centrifugal: All of either fruit or vegetables are fed into the machine onto a fast-spinning grater. The juice is forced through small holes in the grater, while the peel, seeds, etc. stay in the grater or are sent to a waste container that can be emptied when finished. Normally, a jug or cup-type container is supplied with the machine.

Masticating: Here, the fruit and/or vegetables are ground up into a pulp before being forced through a wire mesh with great force. These tend to be quite pricey, but more juice is produced than with a centrifugal machine.

Hydraulic: Here, the fruit and vegetables are chopped and crushed with revolving cutters. They are the most efficient of all, producing the maximum amount of juice, but also the most expensive.

Smoothie machine: These are similar in style to a blender, having a high-sided base where the engine is located and a goblet which has a nondrip pouring spout attached about one-third up from the base. It has tough, durable blades, designed especially for crushing ice and chopping the foods. A pusher is included to ensure that everything is ground and chopped, and they have four push-control buttons. They work efficiently and quickly, producing delicious smoothies in minutes. The goblet has useful measures so you can see at a glance how much you have made. They can be hard to clean, however, and the liquid produced tends to be very thick. It is recommended that you add 300 ml/½ pint liquid (water or juice) to drinks made in this way. Add it early on, along with the first ingredients, so that it sits in the bottom of the machine.

Blender: This can also be called a liquidizer, and consists of a base machine and a goblet with sturdy chopping blades. Often, the goblet has the measurements up the sides and is ideal for soft fruits and vegetables, as well as blending juices with other ingredients. Here, the fruits and vegetables need to be prepared a little more by removing inedible parts, such as stalks, peel, seeds and tough skins. They have speed settings, so look for one that has a good range – many now offer a pulse button, which is an excellent addition.

Cocktail Shaker: Can be used to make non-alcoholic cocktails and some of the drinks found in the Party Drinks chapter. A cocktail shaker has two uses: it combines the ingredients quickly and easily, as well as chilling the drink when shaken with ice. Two types include:

Cobbler shaker or standard cocktail shaker: Normally made of three pieces: a metal (usually stainless steel) outside casing, a lid and a tight fitting cap. There is usually a built-in strainer and the inside is often made of glass. Some have a tap on the side for cocktails that do not need straining.

Equipment & Tips

Boston shaker: Similar to a Cobbler Shaker and looks like the shakers used by professional bartenders. Has no strainer and consists of two parts.

∾ Lemon squeezer: The simple lemon squeezer that most people have in their kitchen is vital for making juices and smoothies. It is ideal for squeezing all citrus fruits and is available in a variety of materials: glass, plastic, wood, ceramic and aluminium.

∾ Citrus presser: This is a more powerful lemon/citrus squeezer and consists of a glass jug with a lemon squeezer sitting on top and a handle at the side. It is operated by simply placing half a citrus fruit on the squeezer and pulling down the handle, which operates a rod that presses out the juice into the jug. It is worth investing in if you plan to make a lot of juices.

∾ Knives: Good knives are essential in the preparation of all food. For these recipes, you need a cook's knife with a large, sturdy blade – essential for cutting large, tough vegetables into portions and also for chopping herbs and fruits. You will also need a couple of other knives: a medium knife, which is ideal for cutting fruits such as melon or pineapple, plus of course a small vegetable knife, invaluable for preparing both fruit and vegetables.

∾ Vegetable peeler: This is also extremely useful. I prefer a swivel peeler, as it is quick and easy to use and only removes a minimal amount of peel or skin, thus helping to preserve the nutrients.

∾ Sturdy chopping board:
This is needed both for cutting the fruit and vegetables and for preserving your work surfaces. Do keep a separate chopping board for fruit and vegetables, one for meat and one for fish. It is important to keep all your equipment scrupulously clean, so dishwasher-safe utensils are a great investment.

Tips

As with many things, preparation is often key to ensuring that a good result is achieved when making smoothies and juices. Once you have the right machine and utensils, you are halfway there, but there are a few other pointers that will help you to produce delicious, nutritious drinks.

- First of all, whichever machine you have, do read the instruction booklet that accompanies it. Each machine will have slightly different applications and instructions, so, for a perfect result, read the booklet first and adapt the recipe if need be.

- Sometimes, when making a drink, it will come through too thick or even too thin – both are easy to rectify. If too thick, stir in some extra liquid or crushed ice; if too thin, pass extra fruit or vegetables through the machine and stir into the drink.

- Both fruit and vegetables are better if kept in the refrigerator before using, as this keeps them fresh and enhances their flavour. Always use plump, ripe produce.

- Frost the rim of a glass by rubbing a little citrus juice or water round the rim and dipping in caster sugar, or even salt for a 'sour'.

- Alternatively, you could add extra pieces of fruit or vegetables, cut into shapes, if liked, and wedge on the rim of the glass. Try thinly paring a long strip of citrus zest and hanging from the rim.

- Be adventurous and experiment. Once you are used to your machine, make up your own concoctions and enjoy blending different ingredients with herbs and spices.

Key Ingredients

Detox

❧

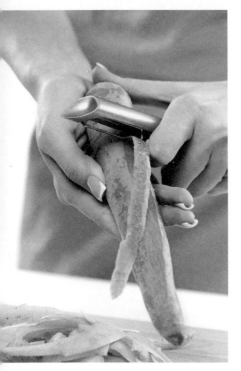

Preparation

When it comes to preparing vegetables, it is recommended to peel root vegetables such as carrots and parsnips, but this is a personal choice and not strictly necessary.

- ❧ Cut off and discard the root if applicable as well as the leaf end and cut into chunks that will easily fit into the machine's goblet.

- ❧ All vegetables, but green vegetables in particular, should be thoroughly washed and allowed to drain.

- ❧ Vegetables should be firm and in good condition, certainly not going rotten and any bruised parts discarded.

- ❧ Use as fresh as possible, as the older the produce, the less of the valuable nutrients it will contain.

The same applies to fruits.

- ❧ Use firm, sound fruits, but do ensure that they are ripe. Underripe fruits will be lacking in taste, flavour and aroma.

- ❧ Citrus fruits should be peeled and the bitter white pith discarded.

- Stones and seeds should be discarded and, where applicable, the fruits should be rinsed and allowed to drain.

- Fruits such as apples and pears can be left unpeeled if preferred, but do discard the core.

- Melons should be skinned and the seeds discarded.

- Pomegranates are better if the flesh and seeds are sieved before using.

- Soft berries such as raspberries should be picked over and leaves or hulls discarded. Lightly rinse before using.

Vegetables

- Beetroot: Use either raw or cooked but not soaked in vinegar. Reputed to help kidney function. Contains folate, potassium and magnesium.

- Broccoli: Use raw. High in fibre and vitamin C, beta-carotene and antioxidants. An important food in the fight against cancer and heart disease.

- Carrot: Peel before using. Rich source of beta-carotene, which converts in the body to vitamin A (good for vision), plus a good antioxidant.

- Celery: Wash thoroughly before use. Helps to lower blood pressure.

- Chilli: Handle with care and, when preparing, avoid touching sensitive parts of the body such as the eyes. Wash hands thoroughly after use. Contains antioxidants, is good for stimulating the metabolic rate and helps to lower blood cholesterol levels. Also contains high levels of capsaicin, a natural painkiller.

Key Ingredients

∞ Courgette: Trim and peel before use. Member of the squash family. Low in calories and a good smoothie base due to high water content.

∞ Cucumber: Part of the squash family. Comes in two varieties – hothouse, the most common, and ridge, a shorter variety with small spikes on the ridged skin. Can act as a mild diuretic and photochemical that can help reduce cholesterol levels in the blood.

∞ Fennel: Also called Florence fennel. Wash thoroughly, discarding the root. Leafy tops can be used as garnish. Contains small amounts of beta-carotene and potassium.

∞ Okra: Also called Lady's Fingers. Trim off the tops before using and use within 1–2 days of purchase. Contains seeds inside the vegetable, which are used as a thickener in Creole dishes. Very good source of soluble fibre, good for lowering cholesterol levels.

∞ Parsnip: Peel and discard top before use and cut into chunks. Flesh has a sweet flavour. Contains a moderate amount of fibre, beta-carotene, vitamin B1 and niacin, essential with the other B vitamins for growth and a healthy nervous system.

∞ Peppers: green, red and yellow Green peppers are one of the best vegetable sources of vitamin C. All peppers are high in beta-carotene as well as rich in vitamin C. As with chillies, all are high in capsaicin, a natural painkiller, and reputed to be helpful in alleviating the pain from arthritis.

∞ Sweet potato: Peel before use. Normally an orange-fleshed tuber, rich in beta-carotene (the white fleshed sweet potato is not). Both varieties contain good quantities of vitamins C and E and are a great source of slow-release carbohydrates.

∞ Tomato: Technically a fruit, tomatoes come in many different shapes, sizes and colours. A rich source of lycopene, an important antioxidant in the prevention of heart disease and cancer. Also contains beta-carotene and vitamins C and E.

Fruits

- **Apple:** Eaters and cookers, normally kept for cooking, come in many varieties. Choose firm, unblemished fruits with plenty of juice. Contains vitamin C. No need to peel but core first.

- **Apricot:** Small, orange-coloured stone fruit with a slightly hairy, edible skin. Needs stoning. High in beta-carotene. Very sweet, especially when dried.

- **Banana:** Skin is green when under-ripe and turns yellow on ripening. Rich in vitamins B6 and C. Popular food as easily eaten and digested. Peel before using.

- **Blackberry:** Grown both wild and cultivated and contains significant amounts of vitamin E, flavonoids and ellagic acid, which helps to block cancer cells. Rinse lightly before using.

- **Blackcurrant:** Rich source of vitamin C and the anti-cancer carotenoid lutein. Grown extensively for commercial juicing rather than sold as fruit. Strip from the stalks, rinse and use.

- **Blueberry:** Small blue/black berries grown in the USA, Italy and France. Rinse before using. Highly nutritious and good in the fight against cancer, especially when dried.

- **Coconut:** Large fruit with a hard, hairy outer casing or husk. To remove from the outer casing, bash with a mallet to reveal the inner fruit. Pierce this carefully to drain off the coconut milk. Coconut is high in saturated fat, although many believe that this fat is not as harmful as animal or dairy saturated fats.

Key Ingredients

✑ Fig: Grown extensively in Mediterranean countries, coming in red, green and purple varieties. Can be eaten fresh or dried. Wash fresh figs before using. Contains small amounts of carbohydrate and beta-carotene.

✑ Grapefruit: Three varieties are available: pink, red and yellow, with yellow being the most common and also more tart than the other two. Contains good amounts of vitamin C. Peel and discard the bitter white pith before using.

✑ Grape: Comes in three colours: green, red and black, both seedless and seeded. Red grapes contain polyphenols, also found in red wine, which help in the fight against heart disease, and some research shows it can help against cancer.

✑ Kiwi fruit: Grown extensively in New Zealand and now available in both green and gold varieties. Small fruits with a brown, slightly hairy skin, the flesh containing tiny edible black seeds. Peel before using. A rich source of vitamin C.

✑ Mango: Grown extensively in India as well as the Caribbean and other tropical countries. A green/yellow smooth skin with bright orange flesh around a large stone. Peel, cut off the flesh and use raw. Very rich in fibre, especially soluble fibre. Helps to keep cholesterol low and also contains vitamin E and antioxidants. Leave until ripe before using.

✑ Melon: About five varieties readily available with perhaps the most popular one being honeydew, with bright yellow skin and pale flesh. Other varieties include ogen, cantaloupe, gallia and watermelon.

✑ Orange: Rich in vitamin C and flavonoids, which have a good antioxidant effect on the body. Peel, discarding the bitter white pith before using.

∾ Papaya: An elongated fruit with a green skin that turns yellow as it ripens. Rich in beta-carotene and an excellent source of soluble fibre, which aids digestion.

∾ Passion fruit: Small, dark purple fruit that wrinkles once ripe. Both the flesh and seeds are edible. Contains vitamin C.

∾ Peach/nectarine: Both members of the same family. Flesh is normally yellow but a white flesh variety is occasionally available during the summer months. Contain vitamin C and a trace of soluble fibre.

∾ Pear: Many English varieties available including Williams, Conference and Comice. Normally picked underripe and allowed to ripen slowly. Contains vitamin C and potassium.

∾ Pineapple: Grown in most tropical and subtropical countries. The attractive plume needs discarding before eating, as do the skin and hard central core. Contains bromelain which aids digestion, breaking down protein and making it easier to digest.

∾ Plum: Many different varieties, including Victoria, Czar, damsons and greengages. All are excellent sources of fibre, with the red-skinned varieties containing beta-carotene.

Key Ingredients

Just Juice

If you're after a delicious drink but you want to try something different from the usual orange juice, why not mix it up with a little pomegranate? For a new clever way of getting vital veggie nutrients into your children, a Celery, Cucumber & Kiwi Fruit concoction will do the trick. Either way this chapter will make your life easier with its healthy refreshments.

Ugli Juice

Serves 1

1 ugli fruit
1 wedge ripe honeydew melon
few black seedless grapes
chilled sparkling water,
to dilute (optional)
extra grapes and mint sprig,
to decorate (optional)

Ugli fruits are similar to grapefruit and are, in fact, a cross between a grapefruit and a tangerine. They are sweeter in taste than the yellow grapefruit, similar to the pink variety. They are quite difficult to find, so snap them up when in season.

Peel the ugli fruit, discarding the peel and pith. Cut the flesh into chunks. Remove any seeds from the melon and discard the skin. Cut into chunks and add to the ugli. Remove the grapes from their stalks and rinse lightly, then add to the rest of the fruit. Pass through a juicer or blender until the juice is formed. Pour into the glass and dilute with water, if using. Decorate the glass with a mint sprig and a few grapes, if using, by hanging little bunches over the rim of the glass.

Alternative
Use either pink or red grapefruit if ugli fruit is not available and, if preferred, strain through a fine sieve to give a smooth juice.

Apple ∞AND∞ Raspberry Juice

Serves 1

2 eating apples,
such as Golden Delicious
225 g/8 oz fresh or
thawed frozen raspberries
150 ml/¼ pint orange juice
ice cubes, to serve
chilled sparkling water,
to dilute (optional)
mint sprig, to decorate

This juice can be made using either fresh or thawed frozen raspberries. If using thawed frozen raspberries, you may find that it produces a little more juice than fresh.

Cut the apples into quarters and discard the cores. Chop into chunks. Pass through a juicer or blender with the raspberries and orange juice (if using a blender) until the juice is formed. Stir in the orange juice if not already used, then pour over ice cubes in glasses and dilute with sparkling water, if using. Float a mint sprig on top and serve.

Alternative
Add a mixture of berries to the apples – try blackberries, strawberries or blueberries.

Berry Juice

Serves 1

175 g/6 oz ripe strawberries
125 g/4 oz ripe raspberries
50 g/2 oz ripe blackberries
ice cubes, to serve
chilled mineral water,
to dilute (optional)
mint sprig and extra berries,
to decorate

Berries such as strawberries, blueberries, blackberries and raspberries are available all year round so there is no need to keep this delicious juice just for the summer months. Strawberries are an excellent source of vitamin C, while raspberries and blackberries are high in fibre and blueberries are reputed to have anti-carcinogenic qualities.

Hull the strawberries, rinse and cut in half. Lightly rinse the raspberries and blackberries. Pass through a juicer or blender until the juice is formed. Place the ice cubes into a glass, pour over the juice, dilute to taste with the water, if using, decorate and serve immediately.

Alternative
Use each fruit separately to make a single flavoured juice. Dilute with iced water if liked in place of the ice cubes. If left for a little while, the juices may need stirring before drinking.

Melon Trio

✾

Serves 2

1 wedge ripe honeydew melon
1 wedge ripe cantaloupe melon
1 wedge ripe ogen melon
small piece root ginger,
peeled and grated
chilled mineral water, to
dilute (optional)
ice cubes, to serve
redcurrant or mint sprigs,
to decorate

These days, we can buy a good variety of melons throughout the year. These range from the red-fleshed watermelon, orange-fleshed charentais, light green ogen and the slightly paler green honeydew, to the similarly pale green to golden gallia and the fragrant orange-fleshed cantaloupe. Vary the juice according to availability and taste.

Discard any seeds from the melon wedges and cut off the skin. Cut the flesh into chunks and pass through a juicer or blender together with the ginger until the juice is formed. Pour into tall glasses, dilute with mineral water, if using, and add ice cubes. Drape redcurrant or mint sprigs over the side and serve immediately.

Alternative
Add 2–3 peeled and seeded clementines to the melons prior to juicing and use a few segments to decorate the glasses.

Melon with Passion Fruit Juice

Serves 1

2 wedges honeydew melon
1 wedge ogen melon
2 ripe passion fruits
chilled sparkling water,
to dilute (optional)
ice cubes, to serve

Passion fruits are at their best when they are at their ugliest. They need to be very wrinkled – if smooth, the fruit will be underripe and the wonderful aromatic flavour will not be at its best.

Discard any seeds from the melon wedges and remove the skin. Cut the flesh into chunks. Scoop out the flesh and seeds from one and a half of the passion fruits and add to the melon flesh. Pass through a juicer or blender until the juice is formed. Pour into the glass. Add sparkling water to dilute, if using, and add ice cubes. Scoop out the seeds from the remaining half of passion fruit and spoon on top of the juices. Serve immediately.

Alternative
Use the flesh and seeds of 3 passion fruits in the juice and top the glasses of juice with a teaspoonful of finely chopped melon flesh.

Mango ~AND~ Orange Juice

Serves 1

2 large ripe mangos
2 large oranges
chilled sparkling water,
to dilute (optional)
ice cubes, to serve
thinly pared orange zest and
mint sprig, to decorate

Mangos provide an excellent source of antioxidant carotenoids and are extremely rich in soluble fibre and a good source of vitamin E. Buy mangos a few days before they are required, as they are best eaten fully ripe.

Peel the mangos and cut the flesh away from the large stone. Cut the flesh into chunks. Using a vegetable peeler, carefully pare off two long thin strips of orange zest and reserve. Peel the remaining zest and bitter white pith off both oranges and divide into segments. Discard the pips and add to the mangos. Pass through a juicer or blender until the juice is formed. Pour into the glass, dilute with water, if using, and add ice cubes. Drape the orange zest down the sides of the glass, add the mint sprig and serve.

Alternative

Canned mangos can be used if ripe ones are not available. Drain before using. Ripe papayas can also be used, but discard the skin and black seeds before juicing.

Tropical Fruit Juice

❀

Serves 2

1 ripe mango
1 papaya
1 ripe passion fruit
½ medium, ripe pineapple
chilled mineral water,
to dilute (optional)
ice cubes, to serve
mint sprigs, to decorate

It is important to ensure that the fruits to be juiced are at their best and perfectly ripe. If beginning to bruise, the fruits may be overripe and the flavour will not be as good.

Peel the mango and cut the flesh away from the stone. Discard the peel and seeds from the papaya and cut into chunks. Add to the mango. Remove the plume and skin from the pineapple and cut lengthways into 4. Discard the hard central core from the pineapple and cut into chunks. Reserve 2–4 pieces of pineapple and add the remainder to the mango and papaya. Pass through a juicer or blender until the juice is formed. Pour into glasses and dilute with water, if using. Add ice cubes and decorate the glasses with the reserved pineapple and mint sprigs. Serve.

Alternative
For a thicker, creamier juice, add 1 large ripe peeled banana before juicing.

Pear ∽AND∽ Raspberry Juice

Serves 1

2 ripe pears, such as
Conference or Comice
1 medium orange
125 g/4 oz fresh or
thawed frozen raspberries
chilled mineral water,
to dilute (optional)
ice cubes, to serve
mint sprig, to decorate
1 tsp crumbled chocolate
flake (optional)

As with all fruits, it is important when eating pears that they are ripe. Otherwise, pears especially lack taste and their texture is woody. Which variety you choose is often a question of taste and familiarity. Unlike many fruits, pears are not normally sold ripe but need to ripen at home. This can take as long as one week but is well worth the wait.

Peel and core the pears, then peel the orange, discarding the bitter white pith, and divide into segments. Lightly rinse the raspberries, if using fresh, and reserve a few for decoration; add to the pears. Pass through a juicer or blender until the juice is formed. Pour into the glass, dilute with water, if using, add the ice cubes, then decorate. If feeling extra indulgent, sprinkle the top with a little crumbled flaked chocolate.

Alternative
Omit the raspberries and add the flesh and seeds of 3 ripe passion fruits. Whizz until blended, then pass through a fine sieve to remove the seeds.

Red Grape Juice with Apple

❧

Serves 1

175 g/6 oz red seedless grapes
2 green apples
2 tbsp orange juice
chilled sparkling water,
to dilute (optional)
ice cubes, to serve
mint sprig, to decorate

Juice made from red grapes contains the same properties as red wine – polyphenols, an antioxidant and a powerful aid against heart disease, and ellagic acid which has cancer-fighting properties. Both excellent reasons to make this one of your favourites!

Remove the grapes from their stalks and rinse lightly; reserve a few for decoration. Cut the apples into quarters and discard the cores. Rinse if not peeling, then cut into chunks. Add to the grapes together with the orange juice and pass through a juicer or blender until the juice is formed. Pour into the glass and dilute with the water, if using. Add ice cubes, decorate and serve.

Alternative
Use this juice as the basis for a nonalcoholic Pimm's. Pour half the amount of juice into a jug and add some ice cubes. Add pieces of chopped fruits, such as apples, pears, strawberries and peaches, and cucumber, and top up with lemonade. Float some washed mint sprigs on top. Allow to stand for 5 minutes, then stir and serve.

Guava AND Mango Juice

Serves 1

4 ripe guavas
1 large ripe mango
1–2 tsp clear honey (optional)
chilled mineral water, to
dilute (optional)
lemon or lime slices,
to decorate

Guavas can be bought fresh or canned, but wherever possible do use fresh. If using canned, drain well before use. Guavas should be used ripe, so look for fruits that have a light yellow skin and yield when pressed lightly with the fingers.

Peel the guavas, discard the seeds and chop into chunks. Peel the mango and cut the flesh away from the stone. Chop and add to the guavas. Pass through a juicer or blender until the juice is formed. Taste and, if liked, add a little honey. Pour into a tall glass and dilute with water, if using, stir, decorate and serve.

Alternative
Replace the mango with 1 large ripe, peeled, seeded papaya and in place of the iced water, place ice cubes in the glass and pour the juice over before serving.

Orange AND Pomegranate Juice

✤

Serves 2

3 large oranges
2 pomegranates
ice cubes, to serve
chilled mineral water,
to dilute (optional)

Pomegranates are one of the few fruits that are not available all year round, so take advantage of them when in season – normally around Christmas time.

Peel the oranges, discarding the bitter white pith, and cut the flesh into chunks. Cut the pomegranates in half and scoop out all the seeds. Reserve a few seeds, if liked, for decoration. Place the seeds with the oranges and pass through a juicer or blender until juiced. Place some ice cubes in the glasses and pour over the juice. Dilute with water, if using. Scatter with the reserved pomegranate seeds, if using, and serve.

Alternative
Replace the oranges with 2 wedges honeydew melon. Remove the seeds and skin, chop into small chunks and blend with the pomegranate.

Sharon AND Peach Juice

Serves 1

3 ripe Sharon fruits
2 ripe peaches or nectarines
chilled mineral water, to serve
strawberry slices and
blackcurrants, to decorate

Sharon fruits, or persimmon, their original name, are not the best fruits to eat raw if they are not ripe. However, once ripe, they are very sweet and juicy and it is well worth waiting for the fruits to ripen.

Discard the stalk from the Sharon fruits, rinse lightly and chop. Lightly rinse the peaches or nectarines, cut in half, discard the stones and cut into chunks. Add to the Sharon fruits and pass through a juicer or blender until the juice is formed. Dilute with the water and pour into the glass. Decorate and serve immediately.

Alternative
Replace the iced water with 150 ml/¼ pint orange juice.

Apple ⬦AND⬦ Blackberry Juice

Serves 1

2 large eating apples
225 g/8 oz ripe blackberries
1–2 tsp clear honey (optional)
ice cubes, to serve
chilled sparkling water,
to dilute (optional)
2 mint sprigs

Apples and blackberries must be one of the most popular combinations of fruits, but they are rarely used for juices. Look for large, plump blackberries that are bursting with flavour and juice.

Lightly rinse the apples and blackberries. Cut the apples into quarters, discard the core, cut into chunks and add to the blackberries. Pass through a juicer or blender until the juice is formed. Taste and add the honey, if liked. Place the ice cubes in the glass, pour over the juice, dilute with water, if using, decorate with mint sprigs and serve.

Alternative

Replace the blackberries with the same amount of ripe blackcurrants. You may need to increase the amount of honey, depending on how ripe the blackcurrants are.

Watermelon with Ginger

❦

Serves 1

1 large wedge watermelon
small piece fresh root ginger
1 lemon grass stalk
ice cubes, to serve

When using ginger with juices, it is recommended that you use fresh root ginger rather than powdered, as a far better flavour is achieved. Use a small sharp knife to peel the ginger and cut into small chunks.

Discard the skin and pips from the watermelon and cut into chunks. Peel the root ginger, chop and add to the melon. Discard the outer leaves from the lemon grass, chop and add to the melon. Pass through a juicer or blender until the juice is formed. Place ice cubes into a tall glass, pour in the juice and serve.

Alternative

Add the juice and flesh from 2 limes in place of the lemon grass stalk. If a sweeter juice is preferred, add a little clear honey.

Carrot *AND* Orange Juice

Serves 2

225 g/8 oz carrots
2 large oranges
3–4 tbsp mineral water,
to blend (optional)
chilled mineral water,
to dilute
orange slices and flat-leaf
parsley, to decorate

Carrots and oranges are a popular blend of flavours and offer a very healthy choice. The resulting juice is full of vitamin C from the oranges as well as flavonoids, which have antioxidant properties. Carrots also contain a rich source of beta-carotene as well as vitamin A.

Peel the carrots and chop into chunks. Peel and discard the bitter white pith from the oranges and divide into segments. Pass the carrots and orange segments through a juicer or blender until the juice is formed. If using a blender, add 3–4 tablespoons water when blending. Pour into tall glasses, diluting with water, if using, decorate and serve.

Alternative
Increase the amount of carrots to 450 g/1 lb and omit the oranges. Use 150 ml/¼ pint chilled mineral water if using a blender. Use large carrots for speed rather than baby carrots.

Carrot, Beetroot and Apple

Serves 1

225 g/8 oz carrots
125 g/4 oz beetroot
(see note right)
2 Granny Smith apples
1 celery stalk or
½ tsp celery salt (or to taste)
chilled mineral water, to
dilute (optional)
ice cubes, to serve (optional)
celery stalk, for stirring

You can, if you wish, use cooked beetroot in this juice – it is easier and quicker to use than raw and will yield slightly more juice.

Peel the carrots and cut into chunks. Peel the beetroot, discarding the root and stalks, and cut into chunks. Cut the apples into quarters, discard the cores and chop roughly. Add to the carrot and beetroot, along with the trimmed, washed and chopped celery stalk, if using. Pass through a juicer or blender until the juice is formed, adding celery salt to taste if wanted. Pour into the glass, dilute with the water, if using, add ice cubes and serve with a celery stalk for stirring.

Alternative
Omit the apple and celery salt and replace with 3 celery stalks that have been trimmed, washed and chopped.

Tomato Juice

Serves 2

450 g/1 lb ripe tomatoes
pinch sugar
chilled mineral water,
to dilute (optional)
ice cubes, to serve
lemon slices, cherry tomatoes and
basil leaves, to decorate (optional)
few dashes Worcestershire
sauce (optional)

Tomato juice must be the most well-known and popular of all vegetable juices. Apart from being a staple juice which can be used in many different ways, it can also have many different vegetables added to it, giving a vast array of flavours which will suit most tastes. Try doing a little experimenting of your own – by adding chilli, garlic, herbs, curry-style spices, vegetables or even some fruits.

Lightly rinse the tomatoes and roughly chop. Pass through a juicer or blender until the juice is formed, then add sugar to taste and dilute with water, if using. Place a few ice cubes in tall glasses and pour over the tomato juice. Decorate as liked, add the Worcestershire sauce, if using, and serve.

Alternative
Add a little Tabasco sauce in place of the Worcestershire sauce, along with some fresh basil leaves and 2–4 garlic cloves. Or try a selection of fresh herbs: thyme, parsley, rosemary or coriander.

Cucumber, Apple and Mint Juice

Serves 1

2 ridge or
1 hothouse cucumber
freshly ground salt,
to sprinkle (optional)
2 Granny Smith apples
2 tbsp orange juice
chilled mineral water, to
dilute (optional)
few fresh mint sprigs

As a member of the squash family, cucumber is naturally a juicy vegetable. When sprinkled lightly with a little freshly ground salt, a cucumber will become even juicier. There are two main varieties of cucumber available: ridge, which are short and have little prickles down the sides of the skin, or the traditional smooth-skinned hothouse variety. Both will work well here.

Cut off and reserve a few thin slices of cucumber. Peel the remainder, then cut into thick slices and place in a colander and add a twist or two of freshly ground sea salt. Leave for 5–10 minutes. Quarter the apples and discard the cores, then chop. Pass all the ingredients through a juicer or blender until the juice is formed. Pour the juice into the glass, dilute with water, if using, and decorate with the reserved cucumber slices and mint sprigs.

Alternative
Simply place the peeled, chopped cucumber into a smoothie machine or blender with the mint and whizz for 2 minutes. Dilute with chilled water.

Beetroot ɢᴀɴᴅ Orange Juice

Serves 1–2

1 whole raw beetroot complete
with leafy tops, if possible
3 large oranges
3–4 tbsp mineral water,
to blend (optional)
small piece fresh root ginger
orange wedges, to decorate
chilled mineral water, to
dilute (optional)

Beetroot is an often overlooked vegetable, which is a great shame. Even more of a shame is that the leaves of the plant are nearly always thrown away – beetroot leaves provide an excellent source of calcium, iron and beta-carotene.

Discard the root from the beetroot. Peel the beetroot as thinly as possible, cut into chunks and reserve. Wash the beetroot leaves thoroughly and chop. Peel the oranges, discarding the bitter white pith and divide into segments. Peel the root ginger and chop. Pass through a juicer or blender (adding a little water, if blending) until the juice is formed. Pour into glasses, decorate and serve diluted with water if liked.

Alternative
Omit the ginger and replace with five trimmed and chopped spring onions and a few dashes of Worcestershire or Tabasco sauce for a more spicy flavour.

Pepper Medley

❦

Serves 1

1 red pepper
1 yellow pepper
1 orange pepper
1 Jalapeño chilli, deseeded
1 large orange
few fresh parsley leaves,
plus extra for decorating
chilled mineral water,
to dilute (optional)
ice cubes, to serve (optional)

Bell peppers are now as common to us as tomatoes, celery or onions and are readily available in red, yellow, orange or green. Having a sweet flavour, they combine well with most ingredients and are perhaps one of our most versatile vegetables.

Cut all the peppers into quarters and discard the seeds and inner membrane, then chop roughly. Discard the seed membrane from the chilli, then chop. Peel the orange, discarding the bitter white pith, and divide into segments.

Pass all the ingredients (except the decoration, water and ice) through a juicer or blender until the juice is formed, then dilute with the water, if using. Pour into the glass and add ice cubes, decorate and serve.

Alternative
Omit the chilli and use basil in place of the parsley. Whizz the peppers with a little iced water to form a juice. Pour into the glass and dilute with iced water if liked.

Tomato and Celeriac Juice

❦

Serves 1

275 g/10 oz fresh tomatoes
½ celeriac, about 275 g/
10 oz in weight
4 spring onions, trimmed,
plus extra for decoration
chilled mineral water,
to dilute (optional)
2 celery stalks, to serve (optional)
ice cubes, to serve
cherry tomato, to decorate

Look for plump, juicy tomatoes when juicing, as underripe tomatoes will not give a satisfactory result – very little juice with a tart flavour. However, do not be tempted to use badly damaged or overripe tomatoes as, although the yield will be good, the flavour could be seriously impaired.

Lightly rinse the tomatoes, then chop roughly. Peel the celeriac and cut into small chunks. Cut the spring onions into small lengths. Pass all the vegetables through a juicer or blender until the juice is formed. Dilute with the water, if using. Pour into the glass, add a celery stalk for stirring, if using, add the ice cubes, decorate and serve.

Alternative
Add a few dashes of sweet chilli or Tabasco sauce after juicing.

Watercress, Tomato and Leek Juice

Serves 1

125 g/4 oz watercress
225 g/8 oz fresh ripe tomatoes
125 g/4 oz tender leeks
1 medium orange
chilled mineral water, to
dilute (optional)
cherry tomato and thyme sprig,
to decorate

Watercress's clean peppery taste combines well with juicy tomatoes and leeks. It is recommended that young, tender leeks are used to give the best results.

Lightly rinse the watercress and reserve. Rinse the tomatoes, chop and add to the watercress. Trim the leeks, chop roughly and wash thoroughly in cold water. Drain. Peel the orange, discarding the bitter white pith, and divide into segments. Pass through a juicer or blender until the juice is formed, then pour into the glass and dilute with the water, if using. Decorate and serve.

Alternative
Replace the watercress with rocket, sorrel or spinach. Make sure that they are all thoroughly washed and shake vigorously before using.

Celery, Cucumber *AND* Kiwi Fruit

Serves 1

4 celery stalks
1 long hothouse cucumber
2 green kiwi fruits
chilled mineral water, to
dilute (optional)
ice cubes, to serve
celery stalk, for stirring

This cool, green juice is perfect for any time of the day but most especially as a breakfast wake-up call. To get the maximum effect, do ensure that you serve it chilled.

Trim the celery, removing the stringy threads, and chop roughly. Peel the cucumber and discard the seeds, then chop roughly. Scoop out the flesh from the kiwi fruits. Pass all the vegetables through a juicer or blender until the juice is formed, then dilute with the water, if using. Pour into the glass, add the ice cubes and serve with the celery stalk for stirring.

Alternative

Replace the kiwi fruits with the flesh from 1 small melon, discarding the skin and seeds.

Tomato, Avocado and Spring Onion

Serves 2

350 g/12 oz fresh tomatoes
1 ripe avocado
3 tbsp lime juice
4 spring onions
chilled mineral water, to dilute
Worcestershire or Tabasco
sauce, to serve
lime slices, to serve

This juice would make a perfect nonalcoholic cocktail. Serve with some Worcestershire or Tabasco sauce and a twist of lime for a refreshing start to any evening.

Rinse the tomatoes and chop roughly. Peel the avocado, discard the stone, chop into chunks and toss in the lime juice. Trim the spring onions and chop, then add to the tomatoes and avocado. Pass all the ingredients through a juicer or blender until the juice is formed. Dilute with the water. Pour into glasses and serve with Worcestershire or Tabasco sauce and lime slices.

Alternative
Add a small amount of chilli to the ingredients before blending. Take care not to add too much – more can always be added if it is not spicy enough for your taste.

Citrus Crush

❧

Serves 1

1 pink grapefruit
2 satsumas
1 lime
chilled mineral water to
dilute, optional
ice cubes to serve
lemon slice to decorate

Citrus fruits are full of vitamin C and as the body does not store this vitamin, a daily glass of this crush will keep the levels up and help to prevent colds.

Peel the grapefruit, satsumas and lime, discarding any pips and divide into segments. Pass through a juicer or blender until the juice is formed. Dilute with the iced mineral water if using. Pour into glasses, add ice cubes if liked and serve. Decorate the glasses with a lime slice.

Alternative
If a slightly sweeter drink is preferred, add a little clear honey before juicing.

Kiwi Fruit Whizz

Serves 1

2 green kiwi fruits
1 golden kiwi fruit
1 red apple, rinsed
150 ml/¼ pint sparkling water
to dilute, optional
ice cubes to serve
apple slices to decorate

It is now possible to get both green and golden kiwi fruits, and they offer one of the best sources of vitamin C. They are best eaten when the fruit yields slightly when lightly pressed.

Peel the kiwi fruits and chop into large pieces. Cut the apple into quarters and core. Reserve 2–4 slices and roughly chop the remainder. Pass the prepared fruits through a juicer or blender until the juice is formed. Pour into tall glasses and dilute with the water if using. Add ice cubes and decorate the glasses with the apple slices. Serve immediately.

Alternative
If liked, use either green or gold kiwi fruits and add 1 small peeled orange in place of the apple. Decorate with kiwi fruit slices.

Pomelo *and* Orange Crush

Serves 1

1 pomelo
2 large oranges
1–2 tsp clear honey or
to taste
chilled mineral water
to dilute, optional

Pomelos are the largest of the citrus fruits and are similar to grapefruits in both look and taste. They have an extremely thick skin and a bitter, fibrous pulp.

Peel the pomelo, ensuring that all the bitter white pith is discarded. Cut off and reserve two thin slices from one of the oranges. Peel both oranges, discarding the white pith and add to the pomelo flesh. Pass through a juicer or blender until the juice is formed. Stir in the honey to taste and pour into glasses. Dilute with water if using, decorate the glasses with the reserved orange slices and serve.

Alternative
Use other citrus fruits if pomelo is not available and dilute with sparkling water.

Peach Juice with Orange and Plum

༄

Serves 1

4 ripe peaches
4 ripe plums, such as
Victoria plums
1 large orange
chilled sparkling water
to dilute, optional
ice cubes to serve

Peaches or nectarines can be used in this recipe, depending on what is available. Look for the white-fleshed varieties, which are around in the summer. They have a more delicate flavour and often contain more juice.

Cut the peaches and plums in half and discard the stones. Rinse lightly then cut into chunks. Peel the orange, discarding the bitter white pith and any pips. Divide into segments and add to the peaches and plums. Pass through a juicer or blender until the juice is formed. Pour into glasses and dilute with water if liked. Add ice cubes and serve.

Alternative

Omit the orange and add 1–2 drops of almond essence to the peaches and plums before blending.

Pineapple *and* Orange Juice

❧

Serves 1

1 large, ripe pineapple
4 tbsp orange juice
chilled sparkling water to serve
ice cubes to serve

When using pineapples to make juice it is imperative that the fruit is perfectly ripe. To check for ripeness, the fruit should have a good aroma and the leaves from the plume should come away when lightly pulled. Avoid over-ripe or damaged fruits.

Place the pineapple onto a board and cut off and discard the plume and base. Standing the fruit upright, carefully cut away the skin with a sharp knife and discard. Cut the fruit lengthways into four wedges and discard the hard central core. Cut into chunks. Pass through a juicer or blender until the juice is formed. Stir in the orange juice, pour into glasses, dilute with the sparkling water, add ice cubes and serve.

Alternative
Omit the orange juice and for a little extra sweetness add 1–2 tablespoons of clear honey.

Blueberry and Raspberry Juice

Serves 1

300 g/10 oz ripe blueberries
175 g/6 oz fresh or thawed
frozen raspberries
1 medium orange
chilled mineral water
to dilute, optional

Blueberries are very small, dark blue fruits, full of nutritional benefits. Juicing them gives a really deep blue juice, full of flavour and goodness.

Rinse the blueberries and raspberries if fresh. Peel the orange, discarding the skin and bitter white pith, divide into segments and add to the blueberries. Pass through a juicer or blender until the juice is formed. Pour into glasses, dilute with iced water if using and serve.

Alternative
Use two large oranges in place of the raspberries and if wanted omit the honey.

Carrot ~AND~ Red Grapefruit Juice

❧❧❧

Serves 1

300 g/10 oz ripe carrots
2 red grapefruit
3–4 tbsp mineral water
to blend, optional
chilled mineral water
to dilute, optional
ice cubes to serve

Red grapefruit tend to be available all year round these days. If you do have trouble finding them, however, use either pink or the more traditional yellow variety.

Peel the carrots, cut into chunks and reserve. Peel the grapefruits, discard the bitter white pith and divide into segments. Add the segments to the carrots and pass through a juicer or blender – with the water if using a blender – until the juice is formed. Pour the juice into glasses, dilute with water if using, add ice cubes and serve.

Alternative
Add 3–4 tablespoons of natural bio yogurt to the juice for a great breakfast wake-up call.

Tasty Treats and Summer Specials

When you want to indulge while keeping your conscience at bay just skim through these pages and we guarantee you'll be satisfied. Tropical Delight is the perfect refreshment on a hazy summer afternoon while a Passionate Peach Melba Smoothie is the ultimate guilty pleasure. And with a delicious Real Strawberry Milkshake on offer, you'll be desperate to join the party!

Apple ∞AND∞ Peach Smoothie

Serves 1

2 red apples, such as Gala
2 tbsp orange juice
2 ripe peaches
150 ml/¼ pint low-fat
natural yogurt
ice cubes, to serve
orange wedge, to decorate

When making this smoothie, do ensure that the peaches are ripe – if not, the flavour will be slightly impaired. Try using peach flavoured yogurt for a greater depth of flavour.

Cut the apples into quarters and discard the core. Chop, then pour the orange juice over them and reserve. Peel the peaches, if preferred, cut in half and discard the stones. Place all the ingredients to be blended in a smoothie machine or blender. If using a smoothie machine, blend on mix for 15 seconds and then on smooth for 30 seconds. In a blender, blend for 1–2 minutes. Pour into the glass, add ice cubes, decorate and serve.

Alternative
If liked, add 1–2 drops of almond extract and replace the yogurt with orange juice. You could also top the smoothies with a spoonful of yogurt.

Berry Smoothie

Serves 2

450 g/1 lb mixed
summer berries
1 large ripe banana, peeled
6 tbsp frozen strawberry yogurt
extra berries, to decorate

Choose from a selection of summer berries, such as strawberries, blueberries, raspberries or blackberries. Do ensure that they are in peak condition, perfectly ripe and fresh.

Clean the fruits, cutting any larger fruits in half or quarters. Place all the ingredients to be blended in a smoothie machine or blender. If using a smoothie machine, blend on mix for 15 seconds and then on smooth for 30 seconds. In a blender, blend for 1–2 minutes. Pour into tall glasses, decorate the glasses with the berries and serve immediately.

Alternative
Add 6 ice cubes to the berries and banana before blending and, once the ice is crushed, pour into tall glasses and top with a scoop of vanilla ice cream.

Tropical Delight

Serves 1

1 large ripe mango
1 large ripe papaya
2 ripe bananas, peeled and
cut into chunks
juice of ½ lime
2–3 tsp clear honey
300 ml/½ pint coconut milk
ice cubes, to serve
lime slice, to decorate

You can vary the fruits used in this smoothie according to taste and availability. Ensure that the fruits are at their best – ripe and full of flavour and aroma.

Peel the mango and papaya and discard the stone and seeds. Chop the fruits into large chunks and pour over the lime juice, then place all the ingredients to be blended in a smoothie machine or blender. If using a smoothie machine, blend on mix for 15 seconds and then on smooth for 30 seconds. In a blender, blend for 1–2 minutes. Place some ice cubes into a tall glass and add the prepared drink. Decorate and serve immediately.

Alternative
Replace the coconut milk with Greek yogurt and sprinkle the top with a little ground cinnamon.

Passion Fruit *and* Guava Special

Serves 1–2

2 ripe passion fruits
2 ripe guavas
2 Golden Delicious apples
4 scoops good-quality
vanilla ice cream

Use passion fruit juice if fresh fruits are not available or you cannot wait for the fruits to ripen. Do not be tempted to use underripe fruits as the flavour will be seriously impaired.

Scoop the flesh and seeds from the passion fruits and, if liked, sieve to remove the seeds. Discard the seeds from the guavas. Cut the apples into quarters and discard the cores and cut into wedges. Reserve 2 scoops of the ice cream, placing all the other ingredients in a smoothie machine or blender. If using a smoothie machine, blend on mix for 15 seconds and then on smooth for 30 seconds. In a blender, blend for 1–2 minutes. Pour into glasses, top with the remaining ice cream and serve.

Alternative
Use one large, ripe orange in place of the apples, discarding the peel and bitter white pith before chopping into chunks.

Pineapple *and* Raspberry Smoothie

Serves 1

1 medium, ripe pineapple
225 g/8 oz fresh raspberries
150 ml/¼ pint orange juice
6 ice cubes
1 tbsp lightly whipped
cream, to serve
1–2 tsp grated dark chocolate,
to decorate

This smoothie can be enjoyed all year round as both fruits are now readily available. If you are fortunate enough to have your own fruit garden and grow raspberries, this is a great recipe for using the fruits that are not perfect to look at but are ripe and bursting with the summer sun.

Discard the plume and skin from the pineapple and cut lengthways into quarters. Discard the hard central core and cut the flesh into chunks. Reserving 1 raspberry to decorate, place all the ingredients to be blended in a smoothie machine or blender. If using a smoothie machine, blend on mix for 15 seconds and then on smooth for 30 seconds. In a blender, blend for 1–2 minutes. Pour into the glass and top with the cream and raspberry. Sprinkle with the grated chocolate and serve immediately.

Alternative
Omit the orange juice and replace with coconut milk and sprinkle with a little toasted desiccated coconut.

Apricot Nectar

Serves 1

6 fresh ripe apricots
4 scoops good-quality
vanilla ice cream
300 ml/½ pint orange juice
1 tsp toasted flaked almonds,
to serve

When you are feeling like giving yourself an extra-special treat or just need to indulge, then this smoothie is perfect for you. Make and enjoy at leisure.

Lightly rinse the apricots, cut in half and discard the stones. Reserve an apricot slice for decoration, if liked, as well as 2 scoops of the ice cream. Place all the other ingredients to be blended in a smoothie machine or blender. If using a smoothie machine, blend on mix for 15 seconds and then on smooth for 30 seconds. In a blender, blend for 1–2 minutes. Pour into the glass, top with the remaining ice cream, sprinkle with the flaked almonds and serve.

Alternative
Use peaches or nectarines in place of the apricots and add 1–2 drops of almond extract.

Cool Raspberry Soda

Serves 2

450 g/1 lb fresh raspberries
1–2 tsp clear honey
4 tbsp orange juice
6 ice cubes
soda water, to serve
2–4 scoops raspberry ripple
ice cream, to serve

If you are fortunate enough to have a pick-your-own fruit farm near you, look for one of the many berries that are available in small outlets. Loganberries, boysenberries or tayberries are the ones you are most likely to find, and they would make a delicious substitute for the raspberries in this recipe.

Hull and clean the raspberries, if necessary, reserve a few for decoration. Place all the ingredients to be blended in a smoothie machine or blender. If using a smoothie machine, blend on mix for 15 seconds and then on smooth for 30 seconds. In a blender, blend for 1–2 minutes. Pour into glasses, top up with soda water, add a scoop of ice cream to each, decorate and serve immediately.

Alternative
Replace the raspberries with fresh strawberries, cutting them in half, if large, and use strawberry ice cream.

Banana with Ginger Cream

❀

Serves 2

2 large ripe bananas
2 large oranges
300 ml/½ pint coconut milk
6 ice cubes
2 tbsp whipped double cream,
to serve
1 tsp ginger
(grated fresh root or ground),
to decorate
1 tsp crystallized ginger,
chopped, to decorate

There are many forms of ginger available, ranging from fresh root ginger and ground ginger to stem and crystallized ginger, which are far sweeter. Use whichever you prefer when making the cream for this recipe.

Peel the bananas and cut into chunks. Peel the oranges, discard the pith and divide into segments. Place all the ingredients to be blended, including the ice, in a smoothie machine or blender. If using a smoothie machine, blend on mix for 15 seconds and then on smooth for 30 seconds. In a blender, blend for 1–2 minutes. Mix the cream and ginger together and stir half into the drink. Pour into glasses, top with the remaining cream and the crystallized ginger and serve.

Alternative
Replace 1 of the bananas with 175 g/6 oz peeled and stoned lychees.

Apricot AND Passion Fruit Lassi

✿

Serves 2

6 ripe apricots
2 ripe passion fruits
125 g/4 oz lychees
150 ml/¼ pint natural yogurt
150 ml/¼ pint apple juice
6 ice cubes
2 lime slices, to decorate

Apricots originate from China but are now widely available when in season. This recipe blends lush, fresh apricots with lychees, aromatic passion fruits and natural yogurt, resulting in an absolutely fabulous drink.

Lightly rinse the apricots and cut in half, discarding the stones. Cut the passion fruits in half and scoop out the seeds and flesh. Sieve the flesh, if preferred. Peel and stone the lychees, then place all the ingredients (including the ice cubes) in a smoothie machine or blender. If using a smoothie machine, blend on mix for 15 seconds and then on smooth for 30 seconds. In a blender, blend for 1–2 minutes. Pour into glasses, decorate and serve immediately.

Alternative
Replace the lychees with 1 ripe peeled banana. If liked, use Greek yogurt in place of the natural yogurt.

Raspberry Pavlova

Serves 2

225 g/8 oz fresh or thawed
frozen raspberries
250 ml/8 fl oz whole or
semi-skimmed milk
2 scoops vanilla ice cream
2 tbsp lightly whipped cream, to serve
2–4 tiny meringues, to serve
2 chocolate-filled rolled wafer
biscuits, to serve

This recipe is based on the very popular dessert of the same name and provides a delicious indulgence, something we all need occasionally. Try it and see.

Place the raspberries, milk and ice cream in a smoothie machine or blender. If using a smoothie machine, blend on mix for 15 seconds and then on smooth for 30 seconds. In a blender, blend for 1–2 minutes. Pour into glasses, top with the whipped cream and crumble over the meringues. Serve immediately with the biscuits.

Alternative
Use other fruits in place of the raspberries – try fresh ripe peaches, nectarines, strawberries or blueberries.

Lemon Meringue Shake

Serves 2

1 tbsp finely grated lemon zest
85 ml/3 fl oz freshly squeezed
lemon juice
1–2 tbsp clear honey, or to taste
450 ml/¾ pint whole or
semi-skimmed milk
2–4 scoops lemon sorbet
2 tbsp lightly whipped cream,
to serve
2 small meringues,
to decorate
thinly pared lemon zest,
to decorate

When using the zest from citrus fruits, wherever possible use organic fruits as these have not been sprayed with chemicals. Organic or not, it is still important that the fruits are thoroughly washed before using the zest.

Place the lemon zest and juice in a smoothie machine or blender and add the honey, milk and sorbet. Whizz for 45 seconds to 1 minute, or until smooth. Pour into glasses and top with the cream. Crumble the meringues and sprinkle over the top, then serve, decorated with the pared lemon zest.

Alternative
Replace the lemon with orange or lime or even all three. Raspberries would also work well, especially if combined with raspberry sorbet.

Orange Flip

Serves 1

2 medium eggs
2–3 tsp clear honey
300 ml/½ pint freshly squeezed
orange juice
2 tbsp freshly squeezed lemon juice
6 ice cubes
orange slice, to decorate

Take care when selecting the eggs for this recipe. Use eggs that are as fresh as possible and, before use, store either in their box or in the egg compartment of the fridge. Allow to come to room temperature for 30 minutes before using. If you are pregnant or have recently recovered from illness, it is recommended that you do not make this drink.

Place all the ingredients in a smoothie machine or blender. If using a smoothie machine, blend on mix for 15 seconds and then on smooth for 30 seconds. In a blender, blend for 1–2 minutes. Pour into the glass, decorate and serve immediately.

Alternative
Replace the orange juice with 300 ml/½ pint blackcurrant juice and top with a spoonful of whipped cream.

Pineapple Smoothie

Serves 1

1 medium, ripe pineapple
2 ripe passion fruits,
flesh and seeds scooped out
1 large ripe banana,
peeled and cut into chunks
300 ml/½ pint natural yogurt
2–3 tsp clear honey
4 ice cubes
2 scoops vanilla ice cream,
to serve
1 tsp grated milk chocolate,
to decorate
maraschino cherry,
to decorate

For this smoothie, you can use either fresh pineapple or pineapple juice: the choice is yours, depending on whether you prefer a smooth drink or if you like the pieces of fruit.

Discard the plume, skin and hard core of the pineapple and cut into chunks. Reserve a little for decoration. Place all the ingredients to be blended, including the ice, in a smoothie machine or blender. If using a smoothie machine, blend on mix for 15 seconds and then on smooth for 30 seconds. In a blender, blend for 1–2 minutes. Pour into the glass, top with the ice cream, decorate and serve.

Alternative
Replace the passion fruit, with strawberries and use strawberry flavoured yogurt.

Strawberry Delight

Serves 2

300 g/11 oz fresh
ripe strawberries
few shakes freshly ground
black pepper
150 ml/¼ pint strawberry yogurt
150 ml/¼ pint natural yogurt
2–4 scoops vanilla ice cream
2 tbsp whipped cream,
to serve
strawberry fans and mint sprigs,
to decorate (optional)

If possible, use locally grown strawberries, as they usually have more flavour than fruit that has been packaged in a supermarket. Try to avoid keeping strawberries in the fridge but, if you have to, remove them at least 30 minutes before using.

Hull then lightly rinse the strawberries and, if large, cut in half. Place all the ingredients to be blended, including the scoops of ice cream, in a smoothie machine or blender. If using a smoothie machine, blend on mix for 15 seconds and then on smooth for 30 seconds. In a blender, blend for 1–2 minutes. Pour into glasses and top with the cream. Decorate each with a strawberry fan and mint sprig, if using.

Alternative
Using freshly ground black pepper with strawberries helps to bring out the flavour. A few drops of balsamic vinegar also has the same effect. If preferred, use a little clear honey.

Apple Crumble Smoothie

Serves 2

3 sweet, juicy eating apples
2 tsp finely grated orange zest
75 ml/3 fl oz apple juice
300 ml/½ pint natural yogurt
150 ml/¼ pint fresh custard
2–4 scoops vanilla ice cream,
to serve
2 digestive biscuits,
to serve
1 tbsp toasted, crushed flaked
almonds and strawberry,
to decorate

Replace a favourite pudding with a smoothie that is simple to prepare, ready in minutes and tastes fantastic. Other fruits can be used instead of apple, much as you can substitute the fruits in a crumble.

Cut the apples into quarters and discard the cores. Chop into chunks and place all the ingredients to be blended in a smoothie machine or blender. If using a smoothie machine, blend on mix for 15 seconds and then on smooth for 30 seconds. In a blender, blend for 1–2 minutes. Pour into glasses and top with the ice cream. Break the biscuits in half and place in the ice cream, sprinkle with the almonds, decorate and serve.

Alternative
Replace the digestive biscuits with a crumbled muesli bar.

Cherry Jubilee

Serves 2

300 g/11 oz fresh ripe
cherries, pitted
75 ml/3 fl oz apple juice
300 ml/½ pint cherry-
flavoured yogurt
6 ice cubes
2 tbsp whipped cream,
to serve
extra cherries and mint sprigs,
to decorate

Cherries are one of the fruits that are only obtainable seasonally, so, when they are around, make the most of them. Although it is not possible to buy frozen cherries, they do freeze reasonably well, so, when in season, buy more than you need and freeze some.

Place all the ingredients to be blended, including the ice cubes, in a smoothie machine or blender. If using a smoothie machine, blend on mix for 15 seconds and then on smooth for 30 seconds. In a blender, blend for 1–2 minutes. Pour into glasses, top with the cream and decorate with the cherries and mint sprigs.

Alternative
Replace the cherries with blackberries and decorate with whole blackberries.

Aromatic Mango Lassi

Serves 2

2 large ripe mangos
4 cardamom pods
1 small piece star anise
2 tsp clear honey
150 ml/¼ pint apple juice
150 ml/¼ pint coconut milk
150 ml/¼ pint natural yogurt
lime wedges, to decorate
cinnamon stick, to stir (optional)

Aromatic spices are widely available in most supermarkets, so add a touch of the Orient to your smoothie. When buying spices, unless you use them often, buy in small quantities, as their aroma and flavour do not last for long. Store them away from the light in airtight containers.

Peel the mangos, cut the flesh away from the stones, cut the flesh into chunks and reserve. Crush the cardamom pods and remove the seeds and discard the pods. Finely crush the star anise. Place all the ingredients to be blended in a smoothie machine or blender. If using a smoothie machine, blend on mix for 15 seconds and then on smooth for 30 seconds. In a blender, blend for 1–2 minutes. Pour into glasses, decorate and serve with the cinnamon stick to stir, if using.

Alternative
Replace the mango with papaya and use orange juice rather than apple.

Banana and Raspberry Smoothie

Serves 1

2 ripe bananas
225 g/8 oz fresh raspberries
75 g/3 oz tofu, drained
150 ml/¼ pint orange juice
4 ice cubes

This nourishing smoothie will help sustain you throughout the day. Not only is it full of energy-rich fruits, it also contains tofu, which will keep you feeling energized.

Peel the bananas and cut into chunks. Place the bananas in a smoothie machine or blender. Reserve a raspberry for decoration, then place all the remaining ingredients into the smoothie machine or blender. If using a smoothie machine, blend on mix for 15 seconds and then on smooth for 45 seconds. In a blender, blend for 1–2 minutes, or until smooth. Pour into the glass, decorate and serve.

Alternative
Other fruits can be used in place of the raspberries – try blueberries, tayberries or loganberries.

Frosty Fruit Smoothie

Serves 2

175 g/6 oz chilled seedless
green grapes
2 ripe passion fruits
½ ripe ogen or cantaloupe melon,
chilled
150 ml/¼ pint chilled apple juice
4 ice cubes

During the summer months when a cold frosty smoothie is called for, it is a good idea to keep a variety of fruits in the refrigerator, so that a refreshing drink can be whizzed up in seconds.

Rinse the grapes and discard any stalks. Reserve a few for decoration and place the rest in a smoothie machine or blender. Scoop the flesh and seeds from the passion fruits, sieve if a smooth texture is preferred and add to the machine. Discard the skin and seeds from the melon and cut into chunks. Place all the remaining ingredients in the machine. Blend in a smoothie machine on mix for 15 seconds and then on smooth for 45 seconds. Or, in a blender, blend for 1–2 minutes until smooth. Pour into cold glasses, decorate and serve.

Alternative
Other chilled juices can be used in place of the apple juice. Apple and cranberry or apple and mango juice work particularly well.

Tropical Fruit Smoothie

Serves 2

1 large ripe avocado
2 tbsp lime juice
1 medium, ripe pineapple
1 tsp clear honey
150 ml/¼ pint chilled
coconut milk
4 ice cubes
2–4 scoops chocolate
ice cream, to serve

Pineapple contains bromelain, which helps to balance the acidity and alkalinity levels in the digestive system. Although coconut milk contains saturated fat, research indicates that it is not nearly as harmful as fat from animal and dairy products.

Peel the avocado, discard the stone, cut the flesh into chunks and sprinkle with the lime juice. Cut the plume and skin off the pineapple and discard. Cut into quarters and discard the hard central core. Cut the flesh into chunks. Place all the ingredients except the ice cream in a smoothie machine or blender. If using a smoothie machine, blend on mix for 15 seconds and then on smooth for 45 seconds. In a blender, blend for 1–2 minutes until smooth. Pour into glasses, top with the ice cream and serve immediately.

Alternative
Omit the pineapple and use any other tropical fruits instead. Papayas, passion fruits or mangos would all work well in this recipe.

Chilled Apple and Blackberry Smoothie

Serves 1–2

2 ripe eating apples
4 tbsp apple juice
150 g/5 oz chilled or frozen ripe
blackberries, plus a few extra
for decoration
300 ml/½ pint natural yogurt
2–4 mint sprigs
2–4 scoops toffee pecan
or vanilla ice cream, to serve
2–4 mint sprigs, to decorate
2–4 ripe blackberries or
2–4 apple wedges, to decorate

Apples are universally popular and have definite health properties. They are full of vitamin C with a low Glycaemia Index, which help to keep hunger pangs at bay.

Rinse the apples, core and cut into chunks. Place the apple juice, chopped apples, blackberries, yogurt and mint in a smoothie machine or blender. If using a smoothie machine, blend on mix for 15 seconds, then switch to smooth for 45 seconds; or whizz in a blender for 1–2 minutes until smooth. Pour into glasses, top with the ice cream and decorate the top with the remaining mint sprigs and ripe blackberries.

Alternative
Raspberries or strawberries can replace the blackberries. If using strawberries, chill rather than freeze, but the raspberries can be chilled or frozen.

Strawberry Slush

Serves 2

450 g/1 lb fresh strawberries,
hulled
1 tbsp balsamic vinegar
3 tbsp orange juice
4 ice cubes
2–4 mint sprigs, to decorate

Strawberries are now readily available all year round, coming from many countries worldwide. When locally grown strawberries are available, use these, however, as the flavour will be far superior to those that have been picked slightly underripe. Locally grown berries are allowed to ripen on the plant, thus enjoying more of the sun, and have much more flavour.

Lightly rinse the strawberries and reserve 2–4 for decoration. Leave the remaining strawberries to drain. Place on a tray and sprinkle with the balsamic vinegar and leave for at least 5 minutes. Place the strawberries and any juice together with the orange juice and ice cubes in a smoothie machine or blender. If using a smoothie machine, blend on mix for 15 seconds and then on smooth for 45 seconds. In a blender, blend for 1–2 minutes until smooth and a 'slush' is formed. Pour into glasses, decorate and serve immediately.

Alternative
Look for white balsamic vinegar in place of the traditional balsamic vinegar, or use a few twists of freshly ground black pepper instead.

Pear ⊰AND⊱ Maple Swirl

Serves 1

2 large ripe dessert pears,
such as William or Conference
1 tsp finely grated orange zest
300 ml/½ pint live natural yogurt
1–2 scoops toffee-flavoured
or vanilla ice cream
orange zest, to decorate
1–2 tbsp maple syrup

This delicious smoothie can be mixed and matched according to personal tastes. We all need a little indulgence occasionally and the maple syrup adds that finishing touch.

Peel and core the pears, chop and place in a smoothie machine or blender with the orange zest and yogurt. Blend on mix for 15 seconds, then switch to smooth for 45 seconds, if using a smoothie machine, or whizz in a blender for 1–2 minutes until smooth. Pour into the glass, top with the ice cream and decorate with the orange zest. Swirl with a little maple syrup and serve immediately.

Alternative
Use chocolate ice cream and swirl with a little melted white chocolate.

Eastern Delight

❧

Serves 2

300 ml/½ pint coconut milk
400 g can lychees, drained
2 cardamom pods
1 lemon grass stalk
1 small piece star anise
2–4 scoops vanilla ice cream,
to serve
2 lemon slices, to decorate

Canned lychees are blended with Eastern spices in this recipe to make an aromatic smoothie with a hint of the Orient.

Place the coconut milk with the drained fruits in a smoothie machine or blender. Place the cardamom pods in a pestle and pound with a mortar to remove the seeds. Place the seeds in the machine. Remove the outer leaves from the lemon grass, chop, then pound with the star anise until as fine as possible. Add to the machine. If using a smoothie machine, blend on mix for 15 seconds and then on smooth for 45 seconds. In a blender, blend for 1–2 minutes, or until smooth. Pour into glasses, top with the ice cream, decorate and serve immediately.

Alternative

You will find that the small pieces of spice will sink to the bottom of the drink, but you can sieve the liquid, if liked. Use live natural yogurt in place of the coconut milk, if preferred.

Almond, Plum and Strawberry Smoothie

❦

Serves 1–2

225g/8 oz ripe plums
300 ml/½ pint bio strawberry yogurt
few drops almond extract
2–3 tsp clear honey,
or to taste
1–2 scoops strawberry or
vanilla ice cream, to serve
1 tbsp toasted flaked almonds,
to decorate
1–2 strawberry slices,
to decorate

Plums offer a good source of fibre. Red plums also contain beta-carotene – the pigment found in foods such as carrots, oranges and dark green vegetables – and an important antioxidant nutrient.

Rinse the plums, cut in half, discard the stones and place in a smoothie machine or blender. Spoon the yogurt into the machine and add the almond extract and honey to taste. If using a smoothie machine, blend on mix for 15 seconds and then on smooth for 45 seconds. In a blender, blend for 1–2 minutes until smooth. Pour into glasses, add a scoop of ice cream to each, sprinkle with the toasted flaked almonds, decorate with the strawberry slices and serve.

Alternative
If fresh plums are not available, use a 400 g can of preserved plums. Drain well and then proceed as above.

Banana Sundae Smoothie

Serves 2

2 ripe bananas
150 ml/¼ pint freshly squeezed
orange juice
300 ml/½ pint coconut milk
4 fresh or dried dates, stoned
and chopped
2 scoops chocolate
ice cream, to serve
2–4 ripe or maraschino
cherries, to serve
1 tsp grated chocolate,
to decorate

When using bananas in smoothies, do ensure that they are ripe. Under-ripe fruits will not blend well with the other ingredients, and the flavour will be impaired.

Cut the bananas into chunks and place all the ingredients except the ice cream, the dates and chocolate in a smoothie machine or blender. If using a smoothie machine, blend on mix for 15 seconds and then on smooth for 45 seconds. In a blender, blend for 1–2 minutes until smooth. Pour into glasses and add a scoop of ice cream to each. Decorate with the cherries and a sprinkle of chocolate and serve.

Alternative
Replace the coconut milk with strawberry-flavoured yogurt and use toffee pecan ice cream.

Passionate Peach Melba Smoothie

Serves 2

1 ripe passion fruit
3 tbsp mango or orange juice
3–4 ripe peaches, stoned
175 g/6 oz fresh or thawed
frozen raspberries
4 scoops vanilla ice cream
2 peach wedges, to decorate
fan wafer biscuits, to serve

Like the dessert of the same name, this smoothie is quick and easy to make and tastes even better than it looks. As with all smoothies, it is important to ensure that the fruit you use is in peak condition.

Cut the passion fruit in half and scoop out the flesh and seeds. Sieve the flesh if a smoother texture is preferred. Place in a smoothie machine or blender and add the mango or orange juice, peaches, raspberries (after reserving 4 or so for decoration) and 2 scoops ice cream. If using a smoothie machine, blend on mix for 15 seconds and then on smooth for 45 seconds. In a blender, blend for 1–2 minutes until smooth. Pour into glasses, add a scoop of ice cream to each, decorate and serve.

Alternative
Make the smoothie as above, omitting the raspberries but adding more peaches and a little more ice cream. Top with the ice cream, drizzle with raspberry coulis and serve immediately.

Real Strawberry Milkshake

Serves 2

225 g/8 oz ripe strawberries
300 ml/½ pint chilled
semi-skimmed milk
4 ice cubes
2 scoops strawberry-flavoured
ice cream, to serve
1 tbsp lightly whipped whipping
or double cream, to serve
2 extra ripe strawberries,
to decorate
mint sprigs, to decorate

Whether or not this transports you back to childhood, once tasted, this fabulous shake will have you hooked.

Hull the strawberries and rinse lightly. Place in a smoothie machine or blender and add the milk and ice cubes. If using a smoothie machine, blend on mix for 15 seconds and then on smooth for 45 seconds. In a blender, blend for 1–2 minutes until smooth. Pour into tall glasses and add a scoop of ice cream to each, top with a little whipped cream and decorate with the extra strawberries and mint sprigs.

Alternative
Other fruits can be used. Try bananas, raspberries, apricots or pineapple, varying the flavour of ice cream accordingly. Or make a chocolate milkshake by omitting the fruits and using 2–3 tablespoons melted chocolate.

Blackcurrant Granita

⋘⋙

Serves 2

225 g/8 oz fresh blackcurrants
75 g/3 oz fresh redcurrants
4 tbsp blackcurrant
cordial or juice
2–3 tsp clear honey, or to taste
1 large or 2 medium juicy
eating apples, such as
Granny Smith
6 ice cubes
orange zest and mint sprigs,
to decorate

When making this granita, turn the freezer setting to rapid freeze in order to speed up the freezing process and obtain the required texture. Do not forget to turn the setting back to normal when finished.

Remove the stalks from the currants and rinse. Place them with the cordial and honey to taste in a smoothie machine or blender. Core the apples and cut into wedges. Add to the machine with the ice. If using a smoothie machine, blend on mix for 15 seconds and then on smooth for 45 seconds. In a blender, blend for 1–2 minutes until smooth. Pour into a freezeable container and freeze for 1 hour, or until slushy. Spoon into glasses, decorate and serve immediately.

Alternative
Look for all three currants, black, red and white, and use an equal amount of each. Add honey to taste.

Detoxing *and* Revitalising

Are you looking for something just that bit healthier, or feeling like you need to cleanse your body with a detox? Well now you can with this selection of invigorating drinks! The Tomato, Celery & Marigold Smoothie will make you wonder what you were waiting for, and if you're looking for a pick-me-up, the Red & Green Whizz will be perfect for you.

Pick-Me-Up Smoothie

Serves 2

2 eating apples
150 ml/¼ pint probiotic
bio live natural yogurt
300 ml/½ pint apple juice
2 rounded tsp
wheatgrass powder
4 ice cubes

If you feel that you are in need of a good pick-me-up, then this smoothie is for you. It contains wheatgrass, an antioxidant with many other health benefits. This smoothie is excellent for vegetarians, as it contains all the B group vitamins.

Cut the apples into quarters, core and chop. Place in a smoothie machine or blender with the yogurt, apple juice, wheatgrass and ice cubes. If using a smoothie machine, blend on mix for 15 seconds and then on smooth for 45 seconds. In a blender, blend for 1–2 minutes until smooth. Pour into glasses and serve.

Alternative
Replace the apple juice with freshly brewed nettle tea, or, if available, add a small handful of fresh, rinsed nettles and filtered water, rather than the nettle tea, before blending.

Watermelon and Flax Oil Smoothie

Serves 1

½ small watermelon
(about 300 g/11 oz in weight
after skin is discarded)
2 large oranges
2 tbsp flax oil
orange wedge, to decorate

Flaxseed is available in capsule form as well as oil, and is a rich source of omega-3 fatty acids. One flaxseed capsule will provide the body's daily requirement.

Remove the watermelon skin, discard the seeds and cut into chunks. Peel the oranges, discarding the bitter white pith, then cut into chunks. Place in a smoothie machine or blender and add the flax oil. If using a smoothie machine, blend on mix for 15 seconds and then on smooth for 45 seconds. In a blender, blend for 1–2 minutes until smooth. Pour into the glass, decorate and serve.

Alternative
Use honeydew or gallia melon if a watermelon is not available.

Carrot *and* Parsley Smoothie

Serves 2

175 g/6 oz carrots, peeled
2 apples, cored
1 hothouse cucumber
150 ml/¼ pint dandelion
and burdock drink
small handful parsley, rinsed
few dandelion leaves, rinsed
150 ml/¼ pint probiotic bio
live natural yogurt
parsley sprig, to decorate

Parsley is a good diuretic; it stimulates the liver and is rich in vitamin C. Try this smoothie if you have overdone the alcohol and have woken up feeling rough. If you are feeling organized, you could collect the ingredients before you go out in the evening and just quickly whizz them together in the morning.

Cut the carrots and apples into chunks and place in a smoothie machine or blender. Peel the cucumber and discard the seeds. Cut 2 slices to use for decoration, chop the rest and place in the machine. Add the dandelion and burdock drink, parsley and dandelion leaves with the yogurt. If using a smoothie machine, blend on mix for 15 seconds and then on smooth for 45 seconds. In a blender, blend for 1–2 minutes until smooth. Pour into glasses, decorate and serve.

Alternative
Replace the dandelion and burdock with green tea and add some milk thistle and burdock leaves, if available.

Tomato, Celery *and* Marigold Smoothie

Serves 2

225 g/8 oz ripe tomatoes
2 eating apples, cored
1 courgette, peeled
few marigold flower heads
and leaves
150 ml/¼ pint unsweetened
apple juice
4 ice cubes
2 extra marigold flowers,
if available, or cherry tomatoes,
to decorate
celery stalk, to stir

Both the flower and leaves of the marigold can be eaten, but do make sure that you wash both thoroughly before use. Marigold is good for cleansing the lymphatic system, liver and gall bladder as well as improving circulation.

Cut the tomatoes, apple and courgette into chunks and place in a smoothie machine or blender with the marigold flowers and leaves. Add the apple juice and ice cubes. If using a smoothie machine, blend on mix for 15 seconds and then on smooth for 45 seconds. In a blender, blend for 1–2 minutes until smooth. Pour into glasses, decorate and serve with a celery stalk for stirring.

Alternative
Replace the marigold flowers and leaves with 2–3 sprigs fresh thyme, also good for improving the circulation.

Watermelon with Kiwi and Echinacea

Serves 1

1 large wedge watermelon
(about ½ a large fruit)
3 kiwi fruits
few drops echinacea tincture
1–2 tsp finely grated
orange zest
4 ice cubes
kiwi slice, to decorate

Echinacea is well known for helping the immune system, but it can also be used to stimulate the lymph glands, help the circulation and purify the blood.

Discard the skin and seeds from the watermelon, cut the flesh into chunks and place in a smoothie machine or blender. Scoop the flesh from the kiwi fruits into the machine and add the echinacea, orange zest and ice cubes. If using a smoothie machine, blend on mix for 15 seconds and then on smooth for 45 seconds. In a blender, blend for 1–2 minutes until smooth. Pour into the glass, decorate and serve.

Alternative
Add the peeled and segmented flesh from 1 large orange and add a small handful chives to help purify the blood.

Banana with Strawberries and Angelica

Serves 2

2 large ripe bananas
350 g/12 oz strawberries
small piece fresh angelica stem or
a few seeds and a couple of leaves
150 ml/¼ pint green tea
1 tbsp rolled oats
4 ice cubes
strawberries and mint sprigs,
to decorate

When using angelica, use washed and dried fresh leaves, seeds or stem, not the candied variety. Angelica tends to be overlooked these days and relegated to the decoration of cakes and desserts. However, if you are lucky enough to have a plant, use the fresh leaves and stems in this delicious drink – good for stimulating the circulation and as a digestive and expectorant.

Peel and chop the bananas and cut the strawberries in half if large. Place in a smoothie machine or blender with the chopped angelica, tea, oats and ice cubes. If using a smoothie machine, blend on mix for 15 seconds and then on smooth for 45 seconds. In a blender, blend for 1–2 minutes until smooth. Pour into glasses, decorate and serve.

Alternative
Omit the bananas and use twice the weight of strawberries, adding an extra tablespoon rolled oats.

Fennel ~AND~ Orange with Aloe Vera

Serves 2

1 large Florence fennel bulb
2 large oranges, peeled
and segmented
1 ridge or ½ hothouse cucumber
25 ml/1 fl oz aloe vera juice
1–2 shakes cayenne pepper
8 ice cubes
cucumber slices, to decorate

Aloe vera has been used throughout the ages to treat infections, allergies and inflammation. It has also been used in treatment for ME, candida and in detoxification. It can be used both orally, as here, and applied to the skin.

Thoroughly wash the fennel and cut into chunks. Place in a smoothie machine or blender, together with the peeled and segmented oranges. Peel the cucumber, discard the seeds, then chop. Add to the machine with the aloe vera, cayenne pepper and ice cubes. If using a smoothie machine, blend on mix for 15 seconds and then on smooth for 45 seconds. In a blender, blend for 1–2 minutes until smooth. Pour into glasses, decorate and serve.

Alternative
Replace the fennel bulb with a head of celery, trimming the stalks and washing thoroughly before use. Reserve the smaller celery stalks with leaves and use to stir the drink.

Fruit Salad Detox Smoothie

❀

Serves 1

150 ml/¼ pint orange juice
1 eating apple
1 ripe peach
small melon wedge
few spinach leaves
small handful flat-leaf parsley
6 ice cubes
parsley sprig and orange wedge,
to decorate

As well as following a detox diet, for maximum benefit it is important to exercise on a regular basis. This helps to increase lymph gland activity and speed up the detox.

Place the orange juice in a smoothie machine or blender. Core the apple and discard the peach stone. Discard the melon skin and seeds. Cut all the fruits into chunks and add to the orange juice with the spinach, parsley and ice cubes. If using a smoothie machine, blend on mix for 15 seconds and then on smooth for 45 seconds. In a blender, blend for 1–2 minutes until smooth. Pour into the glass, decorate and serve.

Alternative
Replace the spinach with rocket or sorrel leaves.

Tomato with Watermelon and Thyme

Serves 1

225 g/8 oz ripe tomatoes
4 tbsp freshly brewed green tea
1 wedge watermelon
(about ½ a large watermelon)
small handful fresh thyme,
plus sprig, to decorate
few whole chive leaves
2–4 ice cubes

Choose plump, ripe and preferably organic tomatoes when making this drink, which is ideal for any time of the day. Thyme is good for counteracting excess sweating problems. Green tea helps in clearing up infections and improves the immune system, as well as helping the fight against heart disease and cancer.

Cut the tomatoes into chunks and place in a smoothie machine or blender with the green tea. Discard the skin and seeds from the watermelon, cut into chunks and add to the tomatoes, together with the thyme, chive leaves and ice cubes. If using a smoothie machine, blend on mix for 15 seconds and then on smooth for 45 seconds. In a blender, blend for 1–2 minutes until smooth. Pour into the glass, decorate and serve.

Alternative
Other melons can be used in place of the watermelon – try ogen or honeydew – and add an additional 150 ml/¼ pint freshly brewed green tea as well.

Strawberry *and* Rosemary Smoothie

✿

Serves 2

350 g/12 oz ripe strawberries
300 ml/½ pint organic bio
live strawberry yogurt
1–2 fresh rosemary sprigs
4 ice cubes
mint sprigs, to decorate

Just because you are following a detox diet, there is no need for the food or drink you consume to be unpleasant. The addition of fresh rosemary with the strawberries in this recipe enhances the memory as well as improving the circulatory system.

Lightly rinse the strawberries, reserve 1 or 2 for decorating and cut the remainder in half. Place in a smoothie machine or blender with the strawberry yogurt. Strip the leaves from the rosemary stalks and add the leaves with the ice cubes to the machine. If using a smoothie machine, blend on mix for 15 seconds and then on smooth for 45 seconds. In a blender, blend for 1–2 minutes until smooth. Pour into glasses, decorate and serve.

Alternative
Try other fruits and flavoured yogurts in place of the strawberries: raspberry, peach or passion fruit with natural yogurt. If using passion fruit, sieve the flesh and seeds before using if a smoother texture is preferred.

Peach ❦AND❧ Passion Fruit Smoothie

Serves 2

2 large ripe peaches
2 ripe passion fruits
150 ml/¼ pint green tea
300 ml/½ pint probiotic bio
live natural yogurt
2 tbsp rolled oats
few fresh basil leaves,
plus extra for decoration
4 ice cubes

When buying peaches or nectarines, choose fruits that feel ripe when lightly pressed and have a good aroma. Fruits which are bought underripe often do not ripen properly and go woody. If your peaches do not appear to be ripening well, poach lightly in a little honey and water. In this recipe, the yogurt will help the digestive system and the rolled oats will help if following a Glycaemic Index diet.

Lightly rinse the peaches, cut in half and discard the stones; reserve 2 slices for decoration. Place in a smoothie machine or blender. Scoop out the passion fruit pulp and seeds and sieve if a smoother texture is preferred. Place in the machine together with the green tea, yogurt, rolled oats, basil and ice cubes. If using a smoothie machine, blend on mix for 15 seconds and then on smooth for 45 seconds. In a blender, blend for 1–2 minutes until smooth. Pour into glasses, decorate and serve.

Alternative
If fresh peaches or nectarines are not available, try using damsons, making sure that all the fruits are sound and not forgetting to discard the stones.

Blueberries with Aloe Vera and Yogurt

Serves 1–2

150 g/5 oz fresh blueberries
25 ml/1 fl oz aloe vera juice
50 ml/2 fl oz elderflower cordial
300 ml/½ pint probiotic bio
live natural yogurt
1 tbsp flax oil
4 ice cubes
mint sprig(s), to decorate

Aloe vera is recognized as helping the body deal with constipation as well as many infections. The juice has a slightly bitter tang, so, by combining it with yogurt in this recipe, the bitterness is not apparent.

Lightly rinse the blueberries, reserve a few for decoration and place the remainder in a smoothie machine or blender with the aloe vera juice, elderflower cordial, yogurt, flax oil and ice cubes. If using a smoothie machine, blend on mix for 15 seconds and then on smooth for 45 seconds. In a blender, blend for 1–2 minutes until smooth. Pour into the glass, decorate and serve.

Alternative
Add 125 g/4 oz raspberries to the blueberries and replace the natural yogurt with bio live raspberry yogurt.

Courgette *and* Cucumber Smoothie

Serves 2

1 whole hothouse cucumber
1 medium courgette
150 ml/¼ pint green tea
300 ml/½ pint probiotic bio
live natural yogurt
few fresh parsley sprigs,
plus extra for decoration
2 fresh tarragon sprigs
4 ice cubes
8–10 whole chive leaves
extra chives leaves,
or 2–4 chive flower heads,
if available, to decorate

Serve this smoothie well chilled for maximum enjoyment: keeping the ingredients in the refrigerator and serving immediately will help. This smoothie is great for dealing with fluid retention.

Peel the cucumber, discard the seeds and cut into chunks. Peel the courgette and cut into chunks. Place all the ingredients, except the decoration, into a smoothie machine or blender. If using a smoothie machine, blend on mix for 15 seconds and then on smooth for 45 seconds. In a blender, blend for 1–2 minutes until smooth. Pour into glasses, decorate and serve.

Alternative
Other herbs that can be used in this recipe that help to relieve fluid retention include parsley, lovage, nettles, dandelion and dock root.

Carrot with Apple and Sunflower Seeds

Serves 2

225 g/8 oz carrots
1 large ripe eating apple
300 ml/½ pint unsweetened
apple juice
1 tbsp sunflower seeds
8 ice cubes

All edible seeds are a good source of energy and minerals.
Both are required when following a detox diet.

Peel the carrots and cut into chunks. Discard the core from
the apple, reserve a slice for decoration and cut the remainder
into chunks. Place in a smoothie machine or blender with
the remaining ingredients, including the ice cubes. If using a
smoothie machine, blend on mix for 15 seconds and then on
smooth for 45 seconds. In a blender, blend for 1–2 minutes
until smooth. Pour into glasses, decorate and serve.

Alternative
Use sesame seeds or flaxseeds in place of the sunflower
seeds, or try a combination of all three.

Beetroot *and* Apple Smoothie

Serves 1

125 g/4 oz beetroot
2 ripe eating apples
small piece fresh root ginger
150 ml/¼ pint apple juice
300 ml/½ pint probiotic bio
live natural yogurt
few shakes cayenne pepper

Try this smoothie to help stimulate the lymphatic system. You can use either raw or cooked beetroot in this recipe. Obviously, using cooked beetroot is far easier than raw, but do ensure that you are using cooked beetroot that has not been steeped in vinegar, otherwise your smoothie will be very tart.

Cut the beetroot into chunks, core the apples and cut into chunks. Peel the ginger and chop. Place in a smoothie machine together with the remaining ingredients. If using a smoothie machine, blend on mix for 15 seconds and then on smooth for 45 seconds. In a blender, blend for 1–2 minutes until smooth. Pour into the glass and serve.

Alternative
Replace the live yogurt with either cranberry or orange juice.

Broccoli with Orange AND Mint

Serves 2

225 g/8 oz broccoli florets
150 ml/¼ pint unsweetened
orange juice
2 large oranges
2–3 fresh mint sprigs
1 tsp flaxseeds
4 ice cubes

Broccoli is an excellent vegetable and provides a good source of fibre and antioxidants, which help in the fight against cancer. Mint is a great detox ingredient, while orange is full of vitamin C. Combined, they offer an extremely healthy and delicious detox drink.

Cut the broccoli into small florets and place in a smoothie machine or blender with the orange juice. Cut a slice from one of the oranges and reserve for decoration. Peel the remaining oranges, discarding the bitter white pith, and divide into segments. Place in the machine with the remaining ingredients. If using a smoothie machine, blend on mix for 15 seconds and then on smooth for 45 seconds. In a blender, blend for 1–2 minutes until smooth. Pour the juice into glasses, decorate and serve.

Alternative
Omit the fresh oranges and increase the amount of unsweetened orange juice to 300 ml/½ pint. The smoothie will be thinner and more juice-like if not using fresh oranges.

Tomato, Apple and Basil Smoothie

Serves 1

225 g/8 oz ripe tomatoes
1 eating apple
2 tsp finely grated orange zest
4 tbsp orange juice
few fresh basil sprigs,
plus extra for decorating
4 ice cubes

This recipe is great when following a detox regime and, provided you use unsweetened apple juice, it will not matter if you use whole apples or juice – both work very well.

Cut the tomatoes into chunks and place in a smoothie machine or blender with all the remaining ingredients. If using a smoothie machine, blend on mix for 15 seconds and then on smooth for 45 seconds. In a blender, blend for 1–2 minutes until smooth. Pour into the glass, decorate and serve.

Alternative
For a speedier drink, replace the fresh tomatoes with one 400 g can chopped tomatoes, then add a few shakes cayenne pepper before whizzing with the other ingredients.

Tomato AND Sweet Pepper Smoothie

Serves 1–2

225 g/8 oz ripe tomatoes
85 ml/3 fl oz freshly
brewed green tea
1 large red pepper, skinned
if preferred
1 small shallot
few basil sprigs
6 ice cubes
cherry tomato and extra
basil leaves, to decorate

Try this smoothie with skinned peppers if time permits. Skinning peppers is easy – simply cut into quarters, discard the seeds and place skin-side uppermost under a preheated grill. Cook for 10 minutes, or until the skins begin to blacken. Allow to cool, then peel them off.

Cut the tomatoes into chunks and place in a smoothie machine together with the green tea. Discard the seeds from the peppers, cut into chunks and add to the tomatoes. Peel the shallot, chop and add to the machine, together with the remaining ingredients. If using a smoothie machine, blend on mix for 15 seconds and then on smooth for 45 seconds. In a blender, blend for 1–2 minutes until smooth. Pour into glasses, decorate and serve.

Alternative
The shallot will give this smoothie a very distinct onion taste – if preferred, replace with chive leaves which, like shallots and onion, will also help combat fluid retention.

Marrow with Avocado and Chilli

Serves 2

½ small marrow
(or use four 2.5 cm/1 in rings)
2 ripe avocados
50 ml/2 fl oz lime juice
300 ml/½ pint orange juice
1 chilli, seeds discarded
4 ice cubes
2 tbsp sour cream or live
natural yogurt, to serve
2 lime slices, to decorate

Avocados can only be bought fresh. Choose plump, undamaged fruits. Allow to ripen in the fruit bowl (not the refrigerator) and, once cut, use immediately. Avocado contains vitamin E as well as other vitamins and minerals that play a good part in reviving the system.

Peel the marrow, discard the seeds and cut into chunks. Cut the avocados in half, peel and discard the stones. Place the marrow, avocado, lime and orange juices, chilli and ice in a smoothie machine or blender. If using a smoothie machine, blend on mix for 15 seconds and then on smooth for 45 seconds. In a blender, blend for 1–2 minutes until smooth. Pour into glasses, top with a spoonful of sour cream or yogurt, decorate and serve.

Alternative
Replace the lime juice with all orange juice for a slightly sweeter drink. Courgettes can be used in place of the marrow.

Sweet Potato with Apple and Chives

Serves 1–2

300 g/11 oz sweet potato
2 celery stalks, trimmed
300 ml/½ pint unsweetened
apple juice
small handful fresh chives,
plus 1–2 tsp snipped chives,
to decorate
6 ice cubes

Sweet potatoes are slightly overlooked by many people, which is a great shame. The sweet orange flesh combines well with many different flavours and, if following a Glycaemic Index diet or just needing a quick pick-me-up, it is an excellent addition to the weekly shopping list.

Peel the sweet potatoes and cut into chunks. Chop the celery, then place both vegetables into a smoothie machine or blender. Add the apple juice and chives with the ice cubes. If using a smoothie machine, blend on mix for 15 seconds and then on smooth for 45 seconds. In a blender, blend for 1–2 minutes until smooth. Pour into glasses, decorate and serve.

Alternative
Yams could be used in place of the sweet potatoes and 2 ripe eating apples with mineral water in place of the apple juice.

Minty Pea *and* Cucumber Smoothie

❦

Serves 2

225 g/8 oz sugar snaps
1 hothouse cucumber,
peeled and cut into chunks
2 celery stalks, chopped
4 spring onions,
trimmed and chopped
150 ml/¼ pint semi-skimmed milk
handful fresh mint
4 ice cubes
chilled mineral water, to dilute
2–3 tbsp live natural
yogurt, to serve
2 cucumber slices and mint
sprigs, to decorate

You can choose how you drink this – either as a deliciously different drink, or a cold, refreshing soup in the summer. Whichever way you choose, it is guaranteed to be very popular.

Place all the ingredients except the mineral water and yogurt in a smoothie machine or blender. If using a smoothie machine, blend on mix for 15 seconds and then on smooth for 45 seconds. In a blender, blend for 1–2 minutes until smooth. Pour into glasses, dilute if preferred, stir in the yogurt, decorate and serve.

Alternative
Use mangetout in place of the sugar snaps and replace the yogurt with a little single cream.

Melon with Blackcurrant and Ginger

Serves 1–2

½ gallia melon
300 ml/½ pint blackcurrant juice or cordial
small piece root ginger
1–2 tsp clear honey (optional)
2 pinches wheatgrass powder
4 ice cubes
mint sprigs, to decorate

Wheatgrass is one of the latest herbs to hit our shelves and has many properties. Among other things, it is an antioxidant and a great booster for the immune system. It comes from wheat grain that is allowed to sprout until it becomes young grass. It is then harvested and ground to form a powder.

Remove the skin and seeds from the melon and cut into chunks. Place in a smoothie machine or blender with the blackcurrant juice. Peel the ginger, chop and add to the machine with the honey, if using, the wheatgrass powder and the ice cubes. If using a smoothie machine, blend on mix for 15 seconds and then on smooth for 45 seconds. In a blender, blend for 1–2 minutes until smooth. Pour into glasses, decorate and serve.

Alternative
Replace the 300 ml/½ pint blackcurrant juice with the same amount of orange juice.

Pear ∽AND∾ Blackcurrant Whizz

Serves 1–2

125 g/4 oz parsnip, peeled
2 ripe pears, such as
Conference, cored
200 ml/7 fl oz blackcurrant
juice or cordial
4 ice cubes
mint sprigs, to decorate

This drink is really quick and easy to make, ready in seconds and guaranteed to refresh instantly.

Cut the parsnip and pears into chunks, reserving 1 or 2 pear slices for decoration. Place the pear and parsnip chunks in a smoothie machine or blender with the blackcurrant juice and ice cubes. If using a smoothie machine, blend on mix for 15 seconds and then on smooth for 45 seconds. In a blender, blend for 1–2 minutes until smooth. Pour into glasses, decorate and serve immediately.

Alternative

Use plump, ripe blackcurrants in place of the juice and swirl with a little live natural yogurt.

Dates with Sweet Potato and Tomatoes

Serves 2

75 g/3 oz fresh or dried dates
225 g/8 oz sweet potato, peeled
175 g/6 oz ripe tomatoes
300 ml/½ pint orange juice
small handful fresh coriander
8 ice cubes
coriander sprigs and cherry
tomatoes, to decorate

Use fresh dates if available: although their carbohydrate content is not as high as dried, they are complemented by the addition of the sweet potatoes.

Cut the dates in half and discard the stones. Cut the sweet potato and tomatoes into chunks and place in a smoothie machine or blender with the dates. Add the orange juice with the coriander and ice cubes. If using a smoothie machine, blend on mix for 15 seconds and then on smooth for 45 seconds. In a blender, blend for 1–2 minutes until smooth. Pour into glasses, decorate and serve.

Alternative
The dates can be replaced with dried or fresh apricots, or use a combination of both.

Melon *and* Elderflower Reviver

Serves 1–2

½ ripe gallia melon
85 ml/3 fl oz elderflower cordial
4 ice cubes
iced sparkling water, to serve
1–2 lemon slices, to decorate

Elderflower has a very delicate flavour and combines well with other fruits such as melon, apple, lemon or lime.

Discard the skin and seeds from the melon, cut into chunks and place in a smoothie machine or blender. Add the elderflower cordial and ice cubes. If using a smoothie machine, blend on mix for 15 seconds and then on smooth for 45 seconds. In a blender, blend for 1–2 minutes until smooth. Pour into glasses and top up with the iced sparkling water. Decorate the glasses with a lemon slice and serve.

Alternative
Try using 2 peeled oranges or 2 cored eating apples in place of the melon.

Grapefruit Refresher

Serves 2

1 red grapefruit
1 pink grapefruit
1 yellow grapefruit
300 ml/½ pint orange juice
1–2 pinches blue-grass
algae powder
8 ice cubes
sparkling water, to dilute
2 each lime slices and
maraschino cherries,
to decorate

It is now possible to buy three different colours of grapefruit: red, pink and the traditional yellow variety. The red and pink are sweeter than the yellow and, by using all three, you will create a refreshing and stimulating drink which should not need any extra sweetness.

Peel all the grapefruits and divide into segments. Place in a smoothie machine or blender with the orange juice, blue-grass algae and ice cubes. If using a smoothie machine, blend on mix for 15 seconds and then on smooth for 45 seconds. In a blender, blend for 1–2 minutes until smooth. Pour into glasses, dilute with water to taste, decorate and serve.

Alternative
Oranges can be used in place of the yellow grapefruit to provide a slightly sweeter drink. Replace the orange juice with grapefruit to give it a little more kick. A little clear honey could be added as well, if liked.

Breakfast Delight

❦

Serves 2

2 pink grapefruits
1 large orange
1 ripe papaya
300 ml/½ pint red grapefruit juice
1–2 tbsp muesli
pinch kelp powder
8 ice cubes
sparkling mineral water, to dilute
mint sprigs, to decorate

Give your system a kick-start with this delicious drink – guaranteed to get you going and keep you going until lunchtime.

Peel the grapefruit and orange and divide into segments. Peel the papaya, discard the seeds and cut into chunks, reserving some for decoration. Place all the fruits with the juice, muesli, kelp powder and ice cubes in a smoothie machine or blender. If using a smoothie machine, blend on mix for 15 seconds and then on smooth for 45 seconds. In a blender, blend for 1–2 minutes until smooth. Pour into glasses, top up with sparkling water, decorate and serve.

Alternative
Replace the muesli with a sugar-free homemade version – rolled oats, a few dried fruits such as raisins or sultanas and a few toasted flaked almonds.

Fig AND Orange Smoothie

Serves 1–2

4–6 ripe fresh figs, depending
on size, or 75 g/3 oz ready-to-eat
dried figs, chopped
150 ml/¼ pint mixed orange
and apple juice
2 large oranges
1 ripe passion fruit
1–2 pinches spirulina powder
4 ice cubes
chilled mineral water, to dilute
orange wedges, to decorate

If using dried figs, look for the ready-to-eat dried figs, as they will blend more quickly than fresh figs. Here, the figs are combined with orange and passion fruit, creating an aromatic and refreshing drink.

Place the figs and fruit juice in a smoothie machine or blender. Peel the oranges, divide into segments and add to the machine. Scoop the flesh and seeds from the passion fruit and add to the machine with the spirulina powder and ice. If using a smoothie machine, blend on mix for 15 seconds and then on smooth for 45 seconds. In a blender, blend for 1–2 minutes until smooth. Pour into glasses, dilute to taste with the mineral water, decorate and serve.

Alternative
The figs can be replaced with ready-to-eat dried or fresh apricots. If using fresh, cut in half and discard the stones, then proceed as above.

Beetroot, Pear and Apple Reviver

Serves 1

125 g/4 oz cooked beetroot
1 eating apple, such as
Granny Smith
1 large ripe pear,
such as Conference
2–3 tsp clear honey
200 ml/7 fl oz apple juice

This great recipe is packed full of energy-giving produce that will help to revive you and keep you going throughout the day.

Cut the beetroot into chunks and place in a smoothie machine or blender. Peel the apple and pear, discard the cores and cut into slices, reserving 1 for decoration. Add the remainder to the machine, together with the honey and apple juice. If using a smoothie machine, blend on mix for 15 seconds and then on smooth for 45 seconds. In a blender, blend for 1–2 minutes until smooth. Pour into the glass, decorate and serve.

Alternative
Replace the apples with oranges and use orange juice instead of the apple juice.

Red *and* Green Whizz

❈

Serves 1–2

125 g/4 oz seedless
red grapes
125 g/4 oz seedless
green grapes
125 g/4 oz ripe cherries
150 ml/¼ pint freshly
brewed ginseng tea
4 ice cubes, to serve

Here, red and green grapes are used with plump, lush cherries, which are bursting with flavour. Cherries have a limited season, so take advantage of them when around and enjoy this fabulous pick-me-up.

Rinse the grapes and reserve a few for decoration. Remove any stalks and then place in a smoothie machine or blender. Stone the cherries and add to the grapes together with the ginseng tea. If using a smoothie machine, blend on mix for 15 seconds and then on smooth for 45 seconds. In a blender, blend for 1–2 minutes until smooth. Place the ice cubes into glasses, add the smoothie, decorate and serve.

Alternative
For a more indulgent drink, top each filled glass with a spoonful of live cherry flavoured yogurt and sprinkle with a little grated chocolate.

Orange with Wheatgrass *and* Yogurt

❦

Serves 1–2

1 large orange
juice of 1 lemon
150 ml/¼ pint orange
or mandarin juice
1 tsp clear honey (optional)
1 pinch wheatgrass powder
150 ml/¼ pint bio live
natural yogurt
4 ice cubes
lemon slice(s), to decorate

Wheatgrass can be used in the diet for a variety of reasons. It acts as a natural tonic to the system as well as being good for detoxification. Here, it is combined with oranges and is perfect for an early morning start.

Peel the orange and divide into segments. Place in a smoothie machine or blender along with the fruit juices, clear honey, if using, and the wheatgrass powder. If using a smoothie machine, blend on mix for 15 seconds and then on smooth for 45 seconds. In a blender, blend for 1–2 minutes. Add the yogurt and ice cubes and whizz for a further 20–40 seconds in a smoothie machine or a further minute in a blender, or until smooth. Pour into glasses, decorate and serve.

Alternative
Replace the orange with 1 pink grapefruit and, if a slightly sweeter drink is preferred, add a little extra honey. Do taste first before adding more honey.

Pomelo ~AND~ Mandarin Smoothie

Serves 1

1 pomelo
3 mandarins
150 ml/¼ pint freshly brewed
green tea
2 tbsp muesli
1 pinch blue-grass algae powder
4 ice cubes
mint sprig, to decorate

Pomelos are the largest of the citrus fruits and have a thick, pale green skin. The flesh is similar to grapefruit, slightly more tart and often in need of a little extra sweetness. Combined with mandarins – small fruits with an easy-to-peel skin and sweet flesh – the flavours balance each other out.

Peel the pomelo, discarding the bitter white pith, and divide into segments. Peel the mandarins, reserving 1 wedge for decoration, and discard pips if necessary. Place both fruits in a smoothie machine or blender, along with the green tea, muesli, blue-grass algae and ice cubes. If using a smoothie machine, blend on mix for 15 seconds and then on smooth for 45 seconds. In a blender, blend for 1–2 minutes until smooth. Pour into the glass, decorate and serve.

Alternative
Use other fruits in place of the pomelo, if liked; try a mixture of pink, red and yellow grapefruit or 1 medium, ripe pineapple.

Kiwi Fruits with Blueberries

❧

Serves 1

2 green kiwi fruits
2 gold kiwi fruits
150 ml/¼ pint bio live
natural yogurt
125 g/4 oz blueberries
1 tbsp flax oil
4 ice cubes
kiwi wedge and a few
blueberries, to decorate

Use either green or gold kiwis or a mixture of both in this drink. Kiwi fruits contain high levels of vitamin C and provide a refreshing, instant pick-me-up when blended into a drink.

Scoop the flesh from each kiwi fruit and place in a smoothie machine or blender along with the remaining ingredients, including the ice cubes. If using a smoothie machine, blend on mix for 15 seconds and then on smooth for 45 seconds. In a blender, blend for 1–2 minutes until smooth. Pour into the glass, decorate and serve.

Alternative
The blueberries can be replaced with raspberries or strawberries, if liked.

Party Drinks

This chapter will provide you with an array of creative drink ideas for any kind of celebration. Try the tropical Hawaiian Island Surfer or treat your tastebuds to the Prohibiton Punch. Why not have some fun and use a cocktail shaker to make some scrumptious, non-alcoholic cocktails, such as a Virgin Raspberry Daquiri.

Strawberry Kiss

✾

Serves 1

3 measures strawberry purée
1½ measures freshly
squeezed orange juice
1 measure freshly
squeezed lemon juice
3 ice cubes, crushed
3–4 measures lemonade
1 tbsp whipped cream
freshly grated chocolate
1 fanned strawberry,
to decorate

If the strawberries that you are using are not that ripe, slice and sprinkle with either a little freshly ground black pepper or balsamic vinegar. Leave for 1–2 hours, then use as directed. The strawberries can also be heated briefly in a microwave; this will help the flavour immensely.

Place the strawberry purée into a cocktail shaker or jug and add the orange and lemon juice. Shake for 20 seconds, or until blended. If using a jug, stir vigorously until thoroughly blended. Place the crushed ice into a tumbler or flute and pour over the strawberry mixture. Top up with the lemonade and float the whipped cream on top. Sprinkle the cream with the chocolate and decorate with a fanned strawberry. Serve with a straw.

Alternative
Try using other flavoured fruit purées; try raspberry, a mixture of berries, mango or papaya.

Hawaiian Island Surfer

❀

Serves 1

2 measures tropical fruit juice
1 measure coconut cream
3 scoops lemon sorbet (or water ice)
4 measures ginger ale
papaya and pineapple wedges and
maraschino cherry, to decorate

Part of the pleasure of a drink, especially at a party, is its look. The decoration should reflect the flavours of the drink itself. Here, the tropical feel is echoed in the use of wedges of papaya and pineapple.

Place the tropical fruit juice into a chilled tumbler or flute and stir in the coconut cream. Add scoops of lemon sorbet (or water ice) and top up with the ginger ale. Thread the fruits on a cocktail stick to decorate and place across the glass. Serve.

Alternative
Use pineapple juice rather than 'tropical' juice, if preferred.

Virgin Raspberry Daiquiri

Serves 1

1 tsp caster sugar
3 measures raspberry syrup
or fresh fruit purée
2 measures pineapple juice
½ measure lemon juice
4 ice cubes, crushed
lemonade, to top up
fresh raspberries threaded
onto a cocktail stick and mint
sprig, to decorate

Alcohol-free cocktails are the perfect answer for underage teenagers. Serve a selection to them, beautifully decorated with straws, umbrellas and pieces of fruit and wow them all.

Place the caster sugar into a saucer and place some water in another saucer. Dip the rim of a chilled glass into the water and then into the sugar. Turn the rim until well coated in the sugar, then chill until required. Pour the raspberry syrup or fresh fruit purée into a cocktail shaker or jug and add the pineapple and lemon juice. Shake or stir until well blended. Place the crushed ice into the sugared glass and pour over the blended drink. Top up with lemonade, decorate and serve.

Alternative
Replace the raspberry syrup with cranberry juice and the pineapple juice with mango juice.

Acapulco Gold

Serves 1

4 ice cubes, crushed
3 measures pineapple juice
1 measure grapefruit juice
1 measure coconut cream
3–4 measures lemonade,
to top up
1 tbsp whipped cream
few coconut flakes and mint sprig,
to decorate

If you have a fresh coconut, it is very easy to make your own coconut flakes. Simply break the fruit in half, reserving the coconut juice inside to add to the drink. Using a swivel vegetable peeler, simply cut off very thin flakes of the fresh coconut. These can be lightly dried out in a warm oven and this will keep the flakes for longer. Remember to store in an airtight container. Fresh flakes should be used within 2–3 days.

Place the crushed ice into a cocktail shaker and pour in the pineapple and grapefruit juice. Add the coconut cream and shake for 20 seconds, or until well blended. Strain into a chilled tumbler and top up with the lemonade. Float the whipped cream on top and serve decorated with the toasted coconut flakes and mint sprig.

Alternative
Try apple juice instead of pineapple juice, if preferred.

Apple of my Eye

❧

Serves 1

3 ice cubes
3 measures clear apple juice
1½ measures blackcurrant syrup
lemonade, to top up
1 scoop good-quality
vanilla ice cream
red eating apple wedge and
blackcurrant sprig, if available,
or mint sprig, to decorate

Blackcurrants, like redcurrants, are one of the few fruits that are not available all year round. Now, when I see them in the shops or markets, I normally buy some and freeze them so that I can use them whenever I want.

Place the ice into a cocktail shaker and pour in the apple juice and blackcurrant syrup. Shake until blended, then strain into a tall tumbler. Top up with the lemonade and place the scoop of ice cream on top. Decorate with the apple wedge, and blackcurrant sprig or mint sprig.

Alternative
Try blending 1 measure whipped cream with the ingredients, rather than floating ice cream on top.

Bora Bora

❧

Serves 1

3 measures pineapple juice
3 measures ginger beer
1 measure coconut cream
1 measure grenadine
½ tsp ground ginger
1 measure freshly squeezed lime juice
1–2 tsp ginger syrup
(use the syrup from a jar of stem ginger)
4 ice cubes, crushed
lime wedges, to decorate

Bora Bora is a Tahitian island that is surrounded by a lagoon and fringing reef. The centre of the island is dominated by the remnants of an extinct volcano, which has two distinct peaks. The word actually means 'peace', which is reflected in the delicious drink below.

Pour the pineapple juice, the ginger beer, coconut cream and grenadine, together with the ground ginger, to taste, the freshly squeezed lime juice and the stem ginger syrup. Shake for 20 seconds, or until well blended. Place the crushed ice into a short tumbler and pour in the prepared cocktail. Decorate with the lime wedges.

Alternative
Top with an extra spoonful of coconut cream and decorate with shavings of fresh coconut.

Brontosaurus

❧

Serves 1

3 measures red grapefruit juice
2 measures freshly
squeezed orange juice
1 measure freshly
squeezed lemon juice
1 measure freshly
squeezed lime juice
½ measure grenadine
4 ice cubes, crushed
2–3 dashes Worcestershire sauce
orange and lemon twists,
plus lime slice, to decorate

The name of the drink actually means 'thunder lizard' in Greek and refers back to when dinosaurs ruled the world. This drink, however, is bang up to date and in the twenty-first century. Perfect any time, day or evening.

Place all the fruit juices into a cocktail shaker with the grenadine and crushed ice. Shake until blended, then pour into a glass and add Worcestershire sauce to taste. Serve decorated with the fruit twists.

Alternative

Replace the grapefruit with carrot juice and add a few dashes of Tabasco sauce to taste. Season with a little freshly ground black pepper and serve with a celery stalk as a stirrer.

Canadian Pride

Serves 1

3 measures pink grapefruit juice
2 measures maple syrup
1½ –2 measures freshly
squeezed lemon juice
1 measure ginger ale
4 ice cubes
lemon zest twist, to decorate

Maple syrup is one of Canada's most famous exports and is used extensively in both food and drinks. It is a sweetener that is made from the sap of the maple tree. It is produced in a sugarbush, or sugarwood – these are wooded shacks where the sap is boiled down to a syrup.

Pour the grapefruit juice with the maple syrup and 1 measure of lemon juice into a cocktail shaker and shake for 30 seconds, or until blended. Check for sweetness and, if necessary, add the remaining lemon juice and shake again. Add the ginger ale and shake briefly. Place the ice into a glass and pour over the drink. Decorate with the lemon zest twist and serve.

Alternative
Try decorating with a slice of grapefruit rather than lemon zest.

Passion Cooler

❦

Serves 1

2 measures freshly
squeezed orange juice
2 measures mango juice
1 measure pineapple juice
1 ripe passion fruit
½ ripe banana, mashed
4 ice cubes, crushed
orange wedges, lime and
pineapple, to decorate

It is best when using passion fruit to buy at least 4 days before you wish to use them. Allow to ripen in the fruit bowl rather than keeping in the refrigerator. It is a matter of personal preference as to whether you use the seeds.

Pour the orange, mango and pineapple juices into a cocktail shaker. Scoop out the seeds and pulp from the passion fruit and place into the cocktail shaker together with the banana. Shake for 30 seconds, or until well blended. Place the crushed ice into a tall tumbler and pour over the blended juice. Thread the fruit wedges onto a cocktail stick and place across the tumbler to decorate.

Alternative
Replace the passion fruit with 1–2 teaspoons grenadine.

Queen Charlie

❦

Serves 1

1 measure grenadine
1 measure guava juice
1 measure mango juice
3 ice cubes
lemonade, to top up
maraschino cherry,
to decorate

If wishing to use a fresh mango to provide the juice for this drink, do make sure that the fruit is ripe and unblemished. Peel, discarding the stone, then whizz in a liquidizer or food processor.

Pour the grenadine into a cocktail shaker together with the guava and mango juices. Add the ice and shake for 30 seconds, or until blended. Pour into a short tumbler and top up with lemonade. Thread the cherry on a cocktail stick and use to decorate the glass.

Alternative
Use other tropical fruit juices according to personal preference and add a mashed banana to make a thicker drink.

Magnificent Peach

✿

Serves 1

2 ripe peaches, stoned
1 measure orange juice
1–2 drops almond essence
3 ice cubes
chilled lemonade, to top up
1 scoop raspberry sorbet
peach and fresh raspberries,
to decorate

This delicious drink is a luscious fruit salad in a glass and is perfect for hot summer days or evenings. Suitable for all ages, it is very easy to vary this recipe by using different flavoured fruit juices.

Slice the peaches and place in a blender or smoothie machine with the orange juice and almond essence. Blend until smooth, then strain into a glass. Add the ice, then pour in the chilled lemonade and top up with a scoop of raspberry sorbet. Place a long-handled spoon into the glass, decorate and serve.

Alternative
The peach can be replaced with nectarines, either the white or yellow fleshed varieties. Use according to personal preference or availability, but do make sure they are ripe.

Tarzan's Juicy Cooler

Serves 1

3 measures freshly squeezed
orange juice
3 measures pineapple juice
½ measure lemon juice
50 g/2 oz ripe strawberries,
lightly rinsed
3 ice cubes
chilled sparkling water,
to top up
1 scoop strawberry ice cream
mint sprig, to decorate

You may not be swinging through the trees after drinking this, but it will certainly keep you cool when the weather gets hot.

Place all the fruit juices into a blender or liquidizer. Reserve 1 of the strawberries for decoration. Slice the remaining strawberries and place into the blender or liquidizer and whizz for 30 seconds. Strain, then pour into a tall tumbler and add the ice cubes. Top up with the chilled sparkling water and float the strawberry ice cream on top. Decorate with the strawberry and mint sprig.

Alternative

Use fresh raspberries and raspberry ripple ice cream in place of the strawberries and strawberry ice cream.

Summer Rain

❦

Serves 1

1 measure freshly
squeezed orange juice
1 measure freshly
squeezed lemon juice
2 measures mango juice
50 g/2 oz fresh ripe
raspberries, lightly rinsed
4 ice cubes
chilled lemonade, to top up
1 scoop lemon sorbet
(or water ice)

When using raspberries in a purée it is always a good idea to sieve the purée afterwards to remove the pips which, if still present, can seriously affect the feel of the drink.

Pour the fruit juices into a blender. Reserve 2–3 raspberries for decoration and add the remainder to the blender. Whizz for 30, seconds or until well blended and then strain. Place the ice cubes into a tall tumbler and pour over the strained drink. Top up with the lemonade and float the lemon sorbet on top. Decorate with the reserved raspberries and serve.

Alternative
Ice cream can replace the sorbet, if liked; try a scoop or two of chocolate ice cream and then sprinkle with a little grated chocolate – delicious or what?

Fruit Flip

Serves 1

1 medium sized orange,
preferably organic
1 ripe lemon,
preferably organic
1 medium organic egg
1–2 tsp, or to taste,
caster sugar
3 ice cubes
orange and lemon twists,
to decorate

It is always best when possible to use organic produce, as they are grown without the aid of artificial fertilizers or pesticides. They can be used with confidence and are guaranteed to be chemical free.

Squeeze out the juice from both the orange and lemon. Whisk the egg with sugar to taste until creamy, then gradually whisk in the orange and lemon juice. Strain into a short tumbler and top up with ice cubes. Decorate with the orange and lemon twists and serve.

Alternative
Replace the lemon with the juice from 1 pink grapefruit. Decorate with a thin slice from the grapefruit and an orange slice.

Pine Lime Sparkle

✳

Serves 1

3 measures pineapple juice
1 measure freshly
squeezed lime juice
2 measures freshly
squeezed lemon juice
1–2 tsp, or to taste, icing sugar
3 ice cubes
chilled lemonade,
to top up
1 small wedge pineapple,
lemon and lime twists,
to decorate

It is recommended that, in order to maintain a healthy lifestyle, we should all eat at least five portions of fruit or vegetables a day. Fruit juice can count as one of your portions. This drink should help you towards your target!

Place the pineapple juice with the lime and lemon juices into a cocktail shaker and add 1 teaspoon icing sugar. Shake for 30 seconds, or until blended. Taste for sweetness and, if necessary, add the remaining icing sugar and shake again. Place the ice into a tall tumbler and pour in the blended juice. Top up with the lemonade and decorate with the pineapple wedge and lemon and lime twists.

Alternative
For a sweeter drink, replace either the lime or lemon juice with orange juice.

Summertime Cooler

❀

Serves 1

50 g/2 oz ripe strawberries, lightly rinsed
50 g/2 oz raspberries, lightly rinsed
1 ripe plum, rinsed, stoned and sliced
1 tsp clear honey
3 ice cubes, crushed
5 measures chilled sparkling water
1 scoop good-quality ice cream
mint sprig, to decorate

If you have a smoothie machine, it can be used for all the fruit-based drinks. It will blend the fruits to a good consistency and ensure that all the valuable fibre is included in the drink.

Place the fruits into a blender together with the honey and whizz for 30 seconds. Rub through a sieve and pour into a tumbler. Add the ice cubes and top up with the chilled sparkling water. Place the scoop of ice cream on top and add a long-handled spoon to the glass. Serve decorated with a mint sprig.

Alternative
Replace the sparkling water with ginger beer, lemonade or soda water. Use lemonade if a sweet drink is required.

Prohibition Punch

❀

Serves 10

1 red apple, rinsed
4–5 mint sprigs
8–10 ice cubes
3 measures sugar syrup
(*see* method)
600 ml/1 pt clear apple juice
300 ml/½ pt cranberry juice
300 ml/½ pt cold freshly brewed
peppermint tea

Prohibition occurred in many countries in the early twentieth century. Most people associate Prohibition with the United States, where it was illegal to sell, make, transport or consume alcohol between 1920 and 1933. This punch would have been ideal to serve then.

Core the apple and chop, then place into a large glass jug, together with the mint sprigs and ice cubes. Pour in the sugar syrup, together with the apple and cranberry juice. Stir in the cold tea, stir well and allow it to stand for at least 20 minutes to allow the flavours to mingle. Serve in short tumblers, ensuring that each glass gets 1–2 pieces of apple.

To make sugar syrup: gently heat 225 g/8 oz white granulated sugar and 150 ml/¼ pint water in a heavy-based saucepan, stirring occasionally, until the sugar has dissolved; bring to the boil and boil steadily (to 105°C/221°F) until a light syrup is formed. Leave to cool, then pour into a screw-top sterilized bottle. When cold, screw down the lid. Use as required.

Alternative
Use blackcurrant cordial in place of the apple juice and decorate the glasses with fresh blackcurrant sprigs, if available.

Spicy Cooler

❀

Serves 10

600 ml/1 pt orange juice
thinly pared zest and juice from
1 lemon, preferably organic
300 ml/½ pt pineapple juice
300 ml/½ pt freshly brewed tea
3–4 tbsp, or to taste, clear honey
small piece root ginger,
peeled and grated
6 whole cloves
2 cinnamon sticks, lightly bruised
1 small orange, preferably organic
10–20 orange wedges, to serve

The addition of spices to this punch infuses it with such
incredible flavour that the alcohol is not missed at all.
Try serving it to your friends and listen to all the praise
they will heap on you.

Add all the ingredients except the small orange and lemon
to a heavy-based saucepan. Heat gently until hot but take
care not to allow the liquid to boil. Thinly slice the orange
and cut into small wedges. Add to the saucepan and heat
for a further 10 minutes. Strain into a heatproof bowl. Serve
either warm or cool, ensuring that each glass gets a wedge
or two of orange.

Alternative
Use light muscovado sugar in place of the clear honey.
Add 1–2 star anise and 3 cracked cardamom pods for
a real taste of the East.

Aromatic Cup

❦

Serves 10

600 ml/1 pt clear apple juice
300 ml/½ pt freshly
brewed green tea
finely peeled zest of 1,
and juice of 2, ripe limes,
preferably organic
6 cardamom pods, cracked
3 whole star anise
2 cinnamon sticks, lightly bruised
½–1 small red chilli, deseeded
2 ripe passion fruits
10 ice cubes
300 ml/½ pt chilled sparkling water
125 g/4 oz lychees,
stoned and chopped
cinnamon sticks,
to serve (optional)

The fragrant aroma of this cup is due to the addition of the star anise, cinnamon sticks, cardamom pods and passion fruit.

Pour the juice and tea into a saucepan. Add the lime zest and juice to the pan with the spices and the chilli. Bring slowly to the boil, then remove from the heat. Scoop out the pulp and seeds from the passion fruits and add to the pan. Cover and leave for at least 1 hour. Strain into a bowl; add the ice, stir in the water and the lychees and serve.

Alternative
Add a little dark muscovado sugar when heating the apple juice. Do remember to remove the spices before serving in glasses.

Barbary Ale

❦

Serves 10

4 large oranges, preferably organic
2 ripe lemons, preferably organic
600 ml/1 pt filtered or mineral water
125 g/4 oz light muscovado sugar
2 tsp ground cinnamon
1½ tsp ground mixed spice
600 ml/1 pt ginger beer
1 lemon, to decorate
10 ice cubes

Muscovado sugar is unrefined sugar with a strong molasses or treacle flavour. It is very dark in colour and slightly sticky.

Thinly peel the rind from 1 of the oranges and squeeze the juice from all the fruit. Place the rind and juices into a heavy-based saucepan. Add the water and sugar. Spoon the cinnamon and spice into a small bowl and blend to a smooth paste with 2 tablespoons water. Stir into the saucepan. Stir frequently over a gentle heat until the sugar has completely dissolved. Continue to heat gently for 15–20 minutes, stirring occasionally, until hot. Remove from the heat and allow to cool for at least 1 hour before straining into a punchbowl. Stir in the ginger beer. Thinly slice the lemon and cut each slice into triangles. Add to the punchbowl with the ice cubes. Serve cold in short tumblers.

Alternative
If ginger beer is not your favourite, replace with lemonade.

Index